Between Two Worlds

Between Two Worlds

My Life as a Child of Deaf Adults

David Sorensen

Gallaudet University Press
Washington, DC

Gallaudet University Press
Washington, DC 20002
http://gupress.gallaudet.edu

Printed in the United States of America

Library of Congress Cataloging-in-Publication Data
Names: Sorensen, David, 1950-
Title: Between two worlds : my life as a child of deaf adults / David Sorensen.
Description: Washington, DC : Gallaudet University, [2019]
Identifiers: LCCN 2018045408| ISBN 9781944838539 (pbk.: alk. paper) | ISBN 9781944838546 (e-book)
Subjects: LCSH: Sorensen, David, 1950- | Children of deaf parents–Biography. | Deaf–Family relationships–United States–Biography.
Classification: LCC HQ759.912 .S67 2019 | DDC 305.9/081–dc23
LC record available at https://lccn.loc.gov/2018045408

∞ This paper meets the requirements of ANSI/NISO Z39.48-1992 (Permanence of Paper).

Contents

Introduction

A Correspondence from My Homeland

Often throughout my adult years, having grown up in a deaf family, I divorced myself, by choice or by happenstance, from the Deaf community altogether. Sometimes, so much of my life has been like living in another country, my family on the opposite shore. It is only now, after thirty-nine years and many life experiences later, that I realize I have come full circle back into the country of Deaf people. I am a hearing child of deaf adults. We are called Codas, and we are our own breed.

Being a Coda within Deaf culture is distinguished by certain roles and characteristics. As the firstborn, my responsibility at an early age was that of an interpreter for my parents, which later was deferred to my younger sister. I was asked my opinion on certain adult decisions such as interpreting medical information. As I became older, I was a confidant to other deaf adults throughout their decision-making processes. Being born within a deaf family had its privileges, namely that I was accepted into the inner circle as a trusted member of the Deaf community even though I was hearing. However, there were limitations there, too. For example, sometimes I was not included, such as at a basketball tournament that permitted only deaf players.

Relations between my father and me and how we communicated (minimally), as well as his discipline style (inconsistent, at times with his belt and other times yelling), were scary and intimidating for a young kid. My attention-seeking and wanting my father's approval or attention, by any means—stealing, lying, through sports, or interpreting—was a dynamic in our relationship. On the other hand, my mother's attempts to discipline were the opposite of my father. She was much more reserved and passive, and she would resort to "wait until your father comes home." The relationship between my parents and the Mormon Church were big influences on the family dynamic, influences that sometimes broke us apart—things that I understand better now. There were times I felt my parents were vacating their roles as parents to attend to the needs of others, to the church, and to my grandmother. My relationship with my sister Christy was difficult at times. She was much younger, and our views differ greatly even today about our deaf parents and our experiences.

But here is what I learned in my home country, through my deaf family: How to teach American Sign Language, which I did at two community colleges in Arizona and Nevada. How to work in group homes for deaf individuals through the community outreach program for the Deaf in Tucson. How to become a teaching assistant at the Oregon School for the Deaf in Salem. How to get myself into graduate school at the University of Arizona. How to work as an educational assistant at the Arizona School for the Deaf and Blind in Tucson. How to counsel deaf individuals in Tucson. How to advocate for deaf services in the Nevada legislature. How to develop a deaf residential treatment program at Desert Hills in Albuquerque. How to work with private nonprofit agencies in developing two group homes for the deaf people, one in San Diego, another in Albuquerque, which was La Familia, which I led as clinical director. How to start my own private practice Southwest Services for the Deaf, in Albuquerque. How to be a strong voice on issues related to deaf people.

By profession, I am a mental health therapist who is fluent in American Sign Language (ASL) and understands Deaf culture. This fluency and cultural understanding allowed me to be trusted, accepted, and valued when I returned to my homeland, the country of Deaf people.

I was born and raised in a deaf family in a time when Deaf culture existed, but was not quite identified yet. Yes, there were schools for deaf people; yes, there was sign language; yes, there were Deaf clubs; and yes, there were national Deaf organizations. However, sign language back then was considered a system of gestures and manual communication, not a bona fide language. There was no Deaf "culture"; there were only a handful of agencies working with deaf populations. Interpreters? What interpreters? Interpreting wasn't a profession; it was a way to "help" deaf people. My family's interpreters were my sister, my fellow Coda comrades, and me. Even the term *Coda* was not invented; we simply said, "MOTHER-FATHER DEAF." Contacting someone? Go next door to the neighbor family's house and use their phone or jump into your car, if you could afford it, and head over to your friend Bob's or Gary's twenty to thirty miles away for a chat. If they weren't home, tough luck; leave a note.

It was not until the late 1950s or early 1960s when the first teletypewriter, or telecommunications device for the deaf (TTY/TDD), was widely used for communication, as long as you could find another deaf individual or family that had a TTY. In the 1960s and 1970s, sign language was finally recognized and verified as a distinct language; it was not a "code" or "version" of English or other spoken languages. Community agencies serving deaf people started springing up everywhere. Research took place at various colleges and universities studying sign language, including the renowned Salk Institute. The Registry of Interpreters for the Deaf, a national certifying agency, was established in 1964. The term *Deaf culture* finally appeared in the 1970s and is now a household term.

Today, the United States has more than 125 interpreter training programs, along with a national interpreting certification. State commissions and agencies are committed to working with deaf people. About 175 residential schools, charter schools, and school programs

for the deaf exist in the United States. Individual communication devices and technologies have gone from the TTY to relay services to videophones and even mobile devices, so that now deaf people can independently make doctor appointments, talk with their attorneys, schedule time to meet with their banks, set up appointments for haircuts, or order pizza. Laws have lessened, somewhat, discrimination at work and created better access for deaf people to programs and services. Most television programs are captioned. And now consider this . . . deaf people now have their own recognized language—American Sign Language, which was the third most-used language in this country, according to a 2006 article in *Sign Language Studies* by Ross E. Mitchell of the Gallaudet Research Institute and colleagues.*
Deaf people have come a long way since the 1950s.

So yes, I am a Coda. I come from that country. Like thousands of other Codas, I consider myself an ambassador between the old-generation deaf and the new-generation deaf.

*Ross E. Mitchell, Travas A. Young, Bellamie Bachleda, and Michael A. Karchmer, "How Many People Use ASL in the United States? Why Estimates Need Updating," *Sign Language Studies* 6, no. 3: 306–35.

PART ONE
Home Country

1

Between Two Worlds

Perhaps the first time I knew I lived in two worlds was when I was seven. I remember one Sunday morning riding in the backseat of my father's car along the narrow two-way road through small town after small town, the familiar way from our California home in Fullerton to Los Angeles, where my family attended church. My father parked our 1953 Chevrolet in its usual curbside spot, forgoing the parking lot, just twenty feet away from the entrance. In the early morning, we were shaded from the warm sun by mature trees lining the street.

It was the custom in our small family to arrive earlier than other church members, but we waited in the car until the service started. I sat with my sister Debbie, who must have been four, as we spoke to each other in English. My parents, known to the fine people of Wilshire Ward Deaf Branch as Melwin David Sorensen and Eileen Richards Sorensen, sat in the front, signing to each other in ASL. I glanced away from Debbie to see what my parents were saying to each other as their hands flew through the air: just a routine, friendly conversation, about the goings-on in the church community. Every once in a while my mother would stop and look back at Debbie and me with a smile before her hands would bolt into action again, continuing her conversation with my father. The two conversations going on in our private family bubble was normal to me: one conversation voiced, the other signed.

Out of the corner of my eye, I noticed two boys about nine and ten approaching our car, then standing about near the back door on the driver's side staring at us. Their eyes were trained on the front seat and not on Debbie nor me. Neither boy wore "church clothing," but they definitely lived in the neighborhood. My voice broke off in the middle of a sentence to follow their gazes; they were gawking at my parents. One boy scrunched his face and raised his hands to mock my parents' signing with indistinct handshapes and gestures, wiggling his fingers and throwing his hands out in front of him. His gestures were wild, incoherent, meaning nothing. The other boy laughed, and the gesturing boy laughed in unison. The entire scene lasted a minute or two at most.

I caught my own face in the rearview mirror. As I saw the bafflement on my face, anger erupted from me. I leaned forward to tap my father and mother on the shoulder and signed, *Look at what those boys are doing!* My mother gave a sidelong glance in their direction, looked at me with a smile, and shrugged it off. Her implication: These boys were not worth her time. I can only assume that these inappropriate expressions were not the only time my parents encountered people mocking them. Although I was angry and puzzled, I followed my mother's lead. Debbie, not really understanding the magnitude of what had just happened, laughed as though it was a fun game.

Mere minutes after the boys had left, we emerged from the car and headed into the church. My parents went in one direction, their Deaf Branch, and I took responsibility for Debbie as we went in another direction to Sunday school with our hearing peers.

2

After the Words

On Christmas Day in 1930, my mother, Eileen Elizabeth Richards, was born in Clarkdale, Arizona, a small farming community about three hours northwest of Phoenix where my grandmother taught elementary school.

Her birthplace couldn't have been more remote. How the family came to Clarkdale was that her father worked for the Arizona Highway Department, and wherever he went, the family followed. They lived in Clarkdale for about two years until my grandparents moved to Littlefield, Arizona, in the Virgin River Valley, along the northwestern border of Arizona and southwestern border of Utah and just south of St. George, Utah, where my grandmother accepted a teaching job. I recall, as a young man, coming up the Virgin River Valley that had shaped my mother's early years. I drove along a plateau when I encountered a highway marker warning of a downgrade for several miles. Once the valley popped into view, I noticed a small community of rural homes dotted with farms. As I approached the valley floor, I saw extensive fields of hay and alfalfa. The Virgin River supplied this farming community with water for agriculture, nourishing it into a lush haven. But forty years ago, this oasis could only be reached by dirt road, another country entirely.

From left, me, Grandma Richards, baby Kyla, and Aaron in my grandmother's front room in Mesa, Arizona.

Her family had spread out all over the map along the border with Arizona, Utah, and Nevada. When my mother was five, the family moved to Boulder City, Nevada, for my grandmother's next teaching assignment. Back then, my grandparents moved to wherever the work was. But one school year later, the family returned to Arizona, moving to Pinedale, a small community in the Mogollon Mountains about 200 miles northeast of Phoenix. There, my grandmother taught for two years in a two-room schoolhouse along with her sister Edna. When it was time for my mother to start school at age six, she enrolled in Pinedale.

The following year, my mother contracted spinal meningitis. She nearly died.

YEARS LATER, she remembered as she signed, *I saw bright lights through a long corridor. There were pretty flowers all around and I felt warm.* I asked my mother if she had been frightened. She answered with a nonchalant expression and signed, *I was never frightened.* Only later did it occur to me to delve deeper, to wonder about how long she had hovered between life and death, to wonder if that was the moment she lost her hearing. Instead, I took in the wonder of her near-passage through the hall of pretty flowers to the other side.

I never told my mother or my father.

She had not died, but she had crossed over into a different world without sound, the world after the words.

MONTHS LATER, AS MY MOTHER CONVALESCED, she had to be carried around because she was too weak to walk. An older female cousin tended to her. My mother remembers no real distress on her parents' part when they discovered that she could no longer hear—though, at seven, it may have been difficult to be truly in tune with the emotional responses of adults. My mother signed to me, *It seemed that my parents realized that I was deaf and that we just had to get used to it.*

My grandparents lived in Pinedale for only a couple years before they moved to Joseph City, Arizona, where my grandfather built their permanent home. It was not until years later, as an adult and out of curiosity, that I visited Pinedale, nestled among the ponderosa pines. The population of Pinedale was not any more than 300 to 400 people. Pinedale, still a sleepy town, probably has not changed much in population over the past seventy-odd years. One thing I noted as I drove through was the schoolhouse where my grandmother had taught. My mother had attended that same school for her first years before she transferred to the Arizona School for the Deaf and the Blind in Tucson.

MY MOTHER WAS postlingually deaf, which means she acquired her spoken language skills before she lost her hearing, so subsequently she had existing speech skills. She had words, but after she became deaf, her words were in one world, and her parents' words were in another. Still, her family expected her to speak, not knowing any other way. She learned how to lipread very well. *My mother and I wrote a lot, whereas my father and I would talk,* she explained. She was comfortable with her mother, who was always available to her. But it was the opposite with her father, who was always gone a few days at a time. My mother seemed resigned to the fact that she was deaf and accepted it as part of her life. She shrugged off the inconvenience. She took it in stride that she had to put forth extra effort to communicate with hearing people by lipreading or writing. However, it was clear when I saw her conversing with other deaf people that she was exuberant and animated. Conversation was easy with them, while it was always a strain to communicate with hearing people.

There came a time when it was obvious to the family that my mother would benefit from being in a school for deaf students. By 1938, my mother's family had settled in Joseph City, east of Flagstaff in northern Arizona, and my grandmother had been hired to teach elementary school. My mother attended fourth grade there until the next school year, when she got into the Arizona School for the Deaf and the Blind in Tucson, about 250 miles away at the opposite end of the state. My mother never knew how her parents learned about the deaf school but suspected the suggestion came from someone in the school district or state's education department.

Through conversations with my grandmother and my mother over the years, I have gleaned that the decision to send my mother to Tucson was by all accounts decided without any discussion with my mother. My grandmother, being an old-school country teacher, believed the school in Joseph City could not provide the education my mother required, especially now that doctors had determined that she was indeed deaf. My grandparents struggled with the decision to send her to the southern part of the state, especially with the obstacles of transportation. When I asked my mother questions about this experience, her response was matter of fact: decisions were made, and she didn't give it much further thought. Naturally, this was the best decision my grandparents could have made.

IN THE FALL OF 1939, my mother began her formal education and acculturation into the Deaf community. I asked her how she felt about leaving her parents and living with people she did not know. She responded, *I do not know. All I knew was I had to learn sign language.* Her own mother attempted to sign but learned only the manual alphabet. Although my grandmother could fingerspell words, she did not understand when someone else fingerspelled to her. My grandfather never learned sign language or how to fingerspell, which my mother simply took as a way of life.

My mother never remembered feeling left out or isolated from her family. However, she enjoyed going home from school, usually via different modes, she told me: by car, but many times by train. She would take the train west to Phoenix, north to Flagstaff, and east to Joseph City.

For return trips, usually only at Christmas or during summer breaks, she often took the bus to Phoenix, and then Aunt Mert, my grandmother's sister, would drive her home. Sometimes my grandparents would come down and pick her up. The next seven years apparently were not very eventful, and she felt that attending the deaf school was no different than any other school. She recalled plenty of friends and getting along well with her teachers and fellow students.

Although my mother was not very athletic and never played sports, she enjoyed watching from the stands. My grandmother told me that my mother was very smart, serving as the class secretary in her junior and senior years as a result of impeccable English and writing skills.

SOON THE TIME CAME for my mother to go to college. The decision to go to Washington, DC, to attend what was then known as Gallaudet College was a foregone conclusion. My grandparents expected my mother to go to college, graduate, and find a secure job. In May 1946, at age fifteen, my mother had done so well at Arizona School for the Deaf and the Blind that she graduated early, and that following fall, she matriculated to Gallaudet, the only major liberal arts college for deaf people in the world.

THERE SEEMED TO BE NO "specialness" over the fact that my mother could not hear, judging from the fact that my grandmother never liked to talk about her feelings or emotions. *My parents never talked about my deafness,* my mother told me. In later years, my grandmother told me she was, indeed, grieved by her daughter's hearing loss.

Only now as an adult can I appreciate what my grandparents went through for my mother, believing their separate lives were in her best interest. Armed with my experience working with deaf individuals in education and agencies providing services for deaf people, growing up in Deaf culture, and being a therapist for deaf individuals, I certainly see things differently. At the time there were few options for my mother. Had I been in their shoes, I would have indeed sent my daughter to Tucson, and on to Gallaudet, though in so many ways, they might as well have been sending their daughter to another world.

3

Like Father, Not Like Son

MELWIN DAVID SORENSEN was my father, and he was truly a sports fanatic. He played many sports, including soccer, baseball, basketball, and volleyball, but boxing was his favorite. When there was a boxing match on television, there was nothing else but that match for him. He had taken up boxing while at the Utah School for the Deaf and the Blind and boxed for a number of years. He won several lightweight class championships, and in his home office, he proudly displayed dozens and dozens of trophies, medals, plaques, and letters of praise on the walls and in specially designed cabinets. Right behind boxing were softball, basketball, and baseball. One Saturday afternoon when I was a young teen, I was watching sports on television with him in our living room in Fullerton, and my father told me he had excelled at baseball in high school enough to go on and play for the local community college, Weber College, in the 1930s.

They offered me a coaching job, he signed and spoke to me simultaneously. I could see vividly both his appreciation and disappointment as he looked at me with his head bent and his face wearing a slight smile. A short moment later, he said, *But I turned it down.*

As he talked about it, he told me the reason was the college had stipulated he live on campus, and he didn't want to live in a residence hall. He had wanted to get married and have kids, and did not want his family to live on campus. But then he added that he thought his being deaf might have been a hindrance.

Do you want to be hearing? I asked.

My father smiled and said he had already gone to doctors to see if there were any surgeries they might be able to perform. He even attempted acupuncture and medications that might help him regain his hearing. *I felt disappointed, but what could I do?* he signed.

At the end of our conversation he cocked his head slightly and glanced up to the side. I understood then that if he could hear, his life would have been a lot different.

MY FATHER WAS BORN in a small farming community in Lovell, Wyoming, on October 29, 1922. He was born at home, as was the custom in those days, to Emanuel and Virginia Sorensen. At age four, my father fell ill to scarlet fever and whooping cough, and became deaf. But it would take months before his parents realized he was deaf, and it would take many more for the full implications to sink in.

MY FATHER WAS A TYPICAL FARM KID, expected to help out with chores such as feeding the animals and working in the sugar beet fields with his father and brothers. As he grew older, his parents knew that the local school would not be able to meet his needs. When my father turned eight, the state of Wyoming wanted to send him to the Montana School for the Deaf and the Blind in Great Falls, since there was no school for deaf children at that time in Wyoming. His parents knew he needed to be sent away to school, but Montana seemed too remote. Instead, they sent him to the Utah School for the Deaf and the Blind in Ogden, a two-day train ride from the farm.

My grandparents were Latter-Day Saints, or Mormons, and felt at ease sending my father to Ogden, which had a large Mormon community. At eight, my father began his formal education at the Utah School for the Deaf and the Blind. At first, his parents, a family member, or another relative would accompany him on the journey to Ogden. As the years passed, my father traveled to and from school alone. Sometimes he would not go home until the following summer, not even during the holidays—just in time to harvest the fields. During those long school years, letters were few and far between. My father was not a letter writer, requiring encouragement from the teachers.

A few times his parents visited him, but there always remained the question of how they would stay connected to their son if he could not hear them. The philosophy at the Utah School for the Deaf and the Blind was like many schools for deaf students of the time. My grandparents were steered to what is called the oral approach, meaning that any form of sign language was forbidden, as was common in those days. The school advised my grandparents to *talk* with him. Never, ever were they to use sign language, as this would delay his language development, according to the professionals. At the school, if students communicated with their hands, they often were disciplined. Yet, my father told me that as kids, when they played and participated in various activities, they would sign to each other behind their teacher's back. Some of the children had deaf parents, so they already knew ASL, and they taught their classmates. Some teachers would sign new vocabulary, even though this was against school policy. Many of the children had developed their own signs to communicate with their families, a common phenomenon in hearing families with deaf children. These "home signs" were more like gestures rather than actual signs, but family members understood each other. Each family had its own home signs independent of other families. But my grandparents were not among those who developed their own home signs, nor did my father's siblings learn and use sign language. As a result, my grandparents never learned to communicate in depth with their deaf son.

MY FATHER OFTEN TOLD ME he was upset with his family for not learning to sign. My numerous observations of the interactions between my father and his brothers or other relatives over the years afforded me some insights. They would approach my father with smiles on their faces, possibly a sign of discomfort or nervousness. They would ask how he was with exaggerated mouthing and facial expressions. I watched the interactions like watching a tennis match, back and forth. My father would smile and attempt to answer them through speech but his gestures were not as exaggerated as theirs. The interactions were always short-lived, possibly due to the hearing people's comfort level. There were times when my father was at a loss and could not understand the conversation, looking to either Debbie or me for help. We often served as his interpreter, and then conversation would flow. I never observed any animosity toward others. Only afterward would my father share with me his frustrations.

My mother, on the other hand, was the quiet one with very little interaction with her in-laws. She was passive and smiled a lot when she interacted with the family, but her conversations were not lengthy. She would always shrug with a smile as if to say, "Oh, well."

ONE PARTICULAR FAMILY REUNION illustrates the dynamic of how we communicated as a family, with some members hearing, some members deaf, some knowing sign language, some called to interpret. It was in 1977, and I had decided to attend after not having seen my family for a while. I was twenty-seven and living in Arizona, and my parents and siblings were living in Fullerton. The family agreed to meet in Salt Lake City. We met at the city park on a warm and cloudless Saturday around ten o'clock in the morning. It was a beautiful park with many mature shade trees. There was a wading pool for the young kids, tennis and basketball courts, and even a sandlot for volleyball. At each picnic area were small BBQ pits for those who wished to cook their chicken, hot dogs, or steaks. There were many families who had the same idea of enjoying the warm summer day. The vast majority of the Sorensens had made the trek from Wyoming, Iowa, California, Arizona, and Utah. Each family had the responsibility of bringing various food and utensils, all put on a table by one side until everyone was ready to eat. Families laid out blankets under the trees, and all the patriarchs and matriarchs gathered under a huge awning to discuss the colors of each family (ours was red). This was to make sure everyone knew where they belonged, and so other Sorensens would know who we were.

I remember watching my parents at the head of the table with the elders, when the colors of the shirts and activities of the day were being discussed. By then I had four younger sisters, and on that day, my sisters and I sat on the periphery listening and observing. Independent of the spoken discussion, my mother and father signed to each other. Since I could understand their signs, they definitely were not talking about the colors of the shirts or the day's events. Occasionally, my parents would look in our direction and smile as if to say, *What's going on?*

"Here we go again," I muttered under my breath to Debbie.

No one asked us to interpret for the family, but Debbie and I decided to go ahead and interpret the conversation, as we often were expected to do. Neither of us wanted to, but we felt compelled.

Throughout most of the day everyone did their thing—play, talk, walk, everyone in their own separate world. Occasionally some family member, a cousin or nephew or a sibling, would come to my parents' table and attempt a conversation. There would be gesturing, exaggerated facial expressions and mouth movements, and the occasional smile, accompanied by head nodding and repeating words. Time and again, I watched my parents' siblings venture in to try to repair some misunderstood communications. At the end of the afternoon, it came time for our ritual when each member of the family stood and took a turn recalling the story of our heritage, when my grandfather came to America from Denmark and when my grandparents met. Uncle Harold was the orator of the family. He was an inventor, a former judge, and a businessman, but in family settings, he was sentimental. As he stood up to speak, my sister Christy said to us, "Oh, my God, I hate it when he talks. He always makes me cry!" Throughout the evening, either Debbie or I interpreted an abridged version of the talk. However, for Uncle Harold's speech, I was the one who signed.

"The Sorensen family is wonderful," he said.

He feels blessed with his immediate family, I signed as I watched my parents and continued to interpret.

I love Mel and Eileen. I wish I could communicate with them directly. I have vowed to learn sign language. And I encourage all of you to learn it, too.

I looked at Christy. She was crying.

I had a sidebar with Debbie, saying, "Oh my God, here he goes again!"

This was the umpteenth time we heard the speech, and we all knew he, or anyone else in the family, would never learn sign language. I asked my parents later during the evening if they felt any family member would follow through. My father looked at my mother and back at me with a grin, making a barely audible sound. All I offered in return was a nod and a smile that told him, "I know."

ONCE SETTLED IN at the Utah School for the Deaf and the Blind, my father proved to be a good student and excelled in all sports. He was very popular with his peers and, as a high school student, always took time to talk with the younger elementary school kids, inspiring awe that a high school student—an athlete no less—would take time to chat with them.

While my father was attending classes at the Utah School for the Deaf and the Blind, he also took classes at Weber College. When he graduated in June 1944, he promptly moved to Southern California mainly to accept the invitation to play basketball for the famed Los Angeles Club for the Deaf (LACD), a social club for deaf people. The LACD organized a basketball team that played against other teams in the area as well as nationally.

The ten years playing starting forward for the LACD were exciting years for my father. Though the players were not paid a salary, they received stipends. He always told me he was not the best shooter; rather, he was known for his ball handling and defensive playing, but I could always sense his pride when he shared these stories.

For the first five years in California, he was single, free to play on the road. He was truly committed to the club and team. I knew this because the only real connection I had with my father was when we talked sports. Those conversations provided me the motivation and heart to play sports as a kid. Looking back now, it seemed I played every sport anyone would let me play: Little League baseball in elementary school and through junior high; football my freshman and junior years in high school; one year of baseball my sophomore year, and track, too; then basketball my sophomore year and briefly my senior year; baseball in city league during the summers of junior high years; and city league softball as an adult. As an adult, I umpired high school baseball, then city league softball.

I wanted to know my father, and so I eagerly talked sports. But this is where it stopped. From elementary school to adulthood, I can count on one hand how many times my father attended any of my games. I tried hard to include him in my life, and thought my playing sports would make him happy. At first I did it for him but eventually I did it for me. I never asked him why he did not attend my practices or games; however, I certainly let him know my team schedule. My junior high coaches and even my neighborhood friends attended many of my games. Then in high school I had community friends, family, and relatives attend my games. When I played in city leagues, many of my friends attended the games. Eventually I let my father know in no uncertain terms through my misbehaviors that I wanted his attention. If I could not do it with sports, I did it through juvenile antics.

ONCE WHEN I WAS thirteen, my father asked me to return a movie at the post office for him. In 1963 there were no DVD or VCR rentals at the local video store, let alone online streaming via Netflix or Amazon. It so happened that the way my parents rented movies was through a monthly movie night at the Deaf club. Although I do not recall the names of the films we saw, I do remember the film itself, wound on a fourteen-inch diameter reel. A person had to place the wheel onto the projector, thread it through, and attach the film to an empty reel, click on the lamp, and start the projector. Only then could we watch the movies on clear white screens.

I gladly accepted this responsibility of returning the movie reel. I took the large package, placed it in the basket on my bike, and rode down the street to the post office. Once I arrived, I was probably third or fourth in line. While in line I chuckled to myself and made a point of not speaking aloud to anyone. The postal clerk signaled it was my turn to approach the counter. I walked up silently and set the large film container on the counter. Across the top of it read *Material for the Deaf.* I stood quietly in front of the clerk as he absorbed the title. He looked up and gave me a blank stare as if to say, "How am I going to talk with this deaf guy?" Well, I thought I would let him squirm. I looked at the man behind the counter with a flat expression. After several moments, I spoke. All the while, I held my face so that it was unreadable. Just act normal, I told myself, but inside I was grinning from ear to ear. Was it mean of me to do this, you think? Probably.

Over the years, I made it a game to feign being deaf. As I started making friends with other children of deaf adults, we would all do it on airplanes, in restaurants, in bars. We went into places and signed. We knew people would stare at us either fascinated with our signing or wondering if we were talking about them. As a younger kid, it was purely mischief on my part. As an adult, my friends and I did silently sign to watch people gawk. Or sometimes we would sign when the surroundings were too loud or when others were talking so we would not interrupt their conversations.

MY DAD HAD STORIES, TOO. The LACD team was not your usual local basketball club. It played professional teams like the Minneapolis Lakers and college teams like the University of Arizona Wildcats. *The season was grueling,* my father would tell me. It was not unusual to play fifty to seventy games a year, traveling by train to cities throughout the United States. One night LACD lost a close game to an Army team starring Ronald Reagan, who was an actor at the time. My father recognized him from such movies as *Dark Victory.* My father's favorites were *Santa Fe Trail* and *Knute Rockne, All American.* In the locker room my father noticed Reagan putting something into his eye. He strolled over to ask Reagan—in both voice and by pointing to his own eye, then to Reagan's eye, with an inquisitive look and a smile—what Reagan put in his eye. The actor showed my father a big clear contact lens. My father had never seen anything like this and asked about it. As Reagan spoke, my father read his lips and learned that this was a contact lens.

The LACD was a well-known club in the 1940s and 1950s, attracting the attention of many star athletes. My father told me proudly about the numerous players who had graduated from Utah and gone on to play for the LACD. The pinnacle of my father's basketball career, as he explained to me, occurred when he and his best friend from school, Paul Loveland, were inducted into the Hall of Fame by the American Athletic Association for the Deaf. My father played basketball for fourteen years until the end of the 1950s.

Upon hearing the stories of my father's basketball career, people have asked me, "Was it hard to be deaf and play basketball, travel, and have a family?" The question always gives me pause. Was it hard being deaf? That depends on whom you ask. There are many variables: Is one rich or poor? What's the personality of the person? What are his intellectual abilities? Is he a highly regarded athlete? Some deaf individuals pull out the "oh poor me card," while others know how to play their cards well. Some accept the fact and go on with it.

Many people who have a disability experience discrimination, oppression, and unemployment/underemployment. However, many deaf people today have a strong sense of identity and pride, and do not like the label *disability.* Still, communication is the number-one barrier between hearing and deaf people. Oftentimes, it is the hearing individual who is challenged about how to interact with those who are "different." Many people are at a loss when it comes to differences: What do I say and do around deaf people? Do I speak to that person? Do I walk on the other side of the street and avoid eye contact? Playing basketball, traveling, and being deaf were all challenges. Travel? My father really did not talk about the drawbacks when he played, other than time away, hustling from one town and hotel room to another for long periods of time. The biggest challenge was, and always has been, communication, especially back then with such limited awareness of

Deaf people and sign language. My father always had a pad of paper and pen or pencil tucked into his shirt pocket. If communication was a challenge, he would pull out the pad and write or ask the other person to write back and forth. Nowadays, with technologies such as FaceTime, videophones, remote interpreting, texting, emailing . . . it is a whole new world and much easier than it used to be.

PART TWO
New Territory

4

Forming a Family

THE FIRST time my mother laid eyes on my father, she was starstruck. *I was fifteen years old and he was handsome and a star basketball player,* she would sign. She never forgot the fall evening in 1946 when she walked into a party after a basketball game between the University of Arizona and the LACD. The Arizona School for the Deaf and the Blind was hosting the victory party, and the room was abuzz. Magic was in the air. That's when her friend introduced her to my father. My mother said she was nervous and felt so hot she could melt like butter.

My father was popular, that was true. She knew he had dated other women. What she liked about my father was that he was *gentle, kind, soft-spoken, and very outgoing. He did not like to gossip like other deaf people. He was not shy or bashful, he loved to talk,* my mother told me, smiling, as we sat in the living room of our home in Fullerton. I had just turned fifty years old, and I had returned to visit her from Albuquerque. My father was now seventy-eight years old. We had just admitted him to a nursing home.

This day had been coming for a while, and my sisters and I knew it. My mother could no longer be his caregiver. My father was over six feet tall and weighed over 220 pounds. My mother was all of five feet two inches tall and more than 100 pounds lighter. Each time my father had fallen, my mother had to call 911. After the third fall, we as a family decided that our father would live in a nursing home. Was there a sense of emptiness or loss? Not so much for my sisters and me, but certainly for my mother. Months later, when I returned in the fall, she would vocalize to me, "I miss Dad," with a sad look on her face.

After that magical meeting between star player and starstruck teen, it was another year and another place before the two met again in 1947 in Washington, DC. The LACD was in the national championship game as hosted by American Athletics Association for the Deaf. When they saw each other again, a long-distance courtship ensued and they wrote each other often. *Every time a letter came from Mel,* my mother told me, *I felt excitement.*

Depending on whom you asked, my father's visit to Joseph City, Arizona, in the summer of 1948 was a big moment—or nothing special. My mother was coy as she told me this. She sat on the couch, and her head shrank into her shoulders as she cocked her head to one side with a sheepish smile. *It went well.*

I asked, *Did your parents like Dad?*

My mother said that her own father had not made much of my father's visit. *My mother told me, he is too old for you. He will be too much of a distraction from your studies.* My mother was eighteen years old.

Distance was not going to keep them apart. In the spring of 1949, my mother visited friends in Los Angeles and saw my father again. Their attraction was most evident, my mother told me. This time, my father persuaded my mother to elope. He knew how her parents felt about him, so he rationalized there was not a better time to marry. She had concerns about what her parents might say, but love tipped the scales and she married him anyway. My grandmother had higher expectations, but my mother had other ideas; she had fallen head-over-heels for my father.

After the elopement, my father's family was thrilled that he had found a woman also raised in the Mormon faith. But my maternal grandmother was furious.

That day as I sat with my mother in the living room, my father now an old man and I, a grown man, we revisited my parents' courtship and marriage. I could still recall the anger I had so often detected in my grandmother's voice. Although my mother may not have been able to hear it—only sense it—I had heard it with my own ears. I could still feel the cadence of Grandma Richards's words as she told me her version of my parents' courtship. The memory sent me back to a day when I was seventeen years old, sitting at Grandma's kitchen table eating breakfast on a Saturday morning.

"Your mother could do better," Grandma said.

We never spoke again on the topic. So there it was, the beginning of my history. In July 1949, Mel Sorensen and the former Eileen Richards eloped and married in the Mormon temple in Los Angeles. Fourteen months later, I was born. It was a late-summer morning, on the eleventh of September in 1950, in Hollywood. I was small, I was cute, and I was their firstborn. Little did these two deaf people know just how rambunctious the sleeping child they held in their arms would be.

I GOT A LOT OF MILEAGE out of that one—declaring I had been born in Hollywood. It wasn't that I knew so many famous stars; instead, it seemed, as the mischievous child of deaf adults, I was a star in my own right, often disrupting the order of things. Or at least that's how it must have seemed to my mother and father when at age three, I struck out from our home in Santa Monica, and walked and walked . . . until a police officer collected me and took me down to the station. The officers kept me entertained with ice cream until my parents arrived. But my father and mother handled me with aplomb. I hardly remember a ripple about this little adventure.

It seems I was good at scaring my parents half to death. As any child would, I tended to investigate small, cozy places. That meant the bathroom and climbing in and out of the kitchen cabinets. One late afternoon when I was two or three, my mother and I were the only ones home. I crawled into one of the cabinets under the sink and closed the door. I fell fast asleep. As I slept, my mother panicked. She frantically searched everywhere—well, almost everywhere. She looked in the bedrooms, the closets, the garage, and the backyard. She ran to our neighbors, who joined the search, fanning out across the neighborhood. This time, my mother knew better than to call the men in blue until she had exhausted all avenues. Meanwhile, I woke up from a peaceful nap, pushed open the cabinet door, and climbed out. I walked outside, where I was greeted by my mother and several of our neighbors on the sidewalk. I thought my mother was having a party. My mother looked rather embarrassed, thanked the neighbors, and waved them off.

FULLERTON, POPULATION 15,000, LIES IN THE HEART of Orange County, California. In March 1955, it was an ocean of orange trees. I remember climbing onto the roof of our home, looking southward into an endless grove of trees. I was in awe, thinking, "What fun!" I saw myself building forts and lobbing oranges like snowballs in fights with my neighborhood pals. We lived on the outskirts of the city center. Fifteen minutes to Disneyland, ten minutes to Knott's Berry Farm.

What brought us to Fullerton, which was thrity-five miles south of Los Angeles, was that my parents needed jobs anywhere they could find them. My mother found work first as a keypunch operator. Not too much later, she moved to Hughes Aircraft, where she worked the swing shift. My father followed, snagging a day-shift job. At home, she covered days, while he covered the nights—sort of, but not really. Most mornings, I was on my own. My mother did not get to bed until two in the morning, which meant she got up after I left for school. While my parents slept or worked, I would get up early and fix myself a simple breakfast of cereal and milk. My day started with *Captain Kangaroo* and Mister Green Jeans and *Our Gang*.

MOST EVERY THURSDAY EVENING, my father's team, the LACD team, played a game. Sometimes the game would be between two deaf teams; most of the time it was against a hearing team. On those nights, my mother prepared dinner, usually chili or beans and we sat down as a family for dinner.

But many nights she did not cook. She instead got ready for work, and we had to fend for ourselves. That left the culinary arts to my dad, not known for his talents in this area. He often threw together a wholesome dinner of bread and milk with a side dish of jam and a small saucer of ringed onions. Some nights, he served stewed tomatoes with sugar. These good ol' dishes were what I considered farm food, comfort food. After dinner, my mom dressed for work while my dad gathered up basketball equipment. Then the night shift would begin: My mother keypunching at Hughes, my father and me driving to Los Angeles for games.

My dad played basketball in a towering fifteen-story building, the lobby of which was lined with glass cases of World War II memorabilia such as German army helmets and rifles with bayonets. A black man, dressed in a neat, well-pressed uniform, operated the elevator. Beneath his hat with a short brim, he smiled and nodded, greeting my father and me. My father used his hands to say the floor number he wanted. The elevator man smiled and pushed the number on a lit console.

On the top floor, the doors opened right onto the basketball court. Ballplayers zoomed through their routines, balls thunking the wood floor, swishing the nets. To the left, the stands buzzed with spectators.

We split—my dad to the lockers, me bounding up the bleachers to find my friends. My comrades and I ran up and down the risers, flying, laughing, playing. We had the run of the gym, and most of the time, I didn't get in trouble.

I became known as the Whistler. My talent was whistling in any of twenty different ways. I was loud, too—so loud that once I stopped the game. All the hearing players on the opposing team froze and the deaf players followed moments later, puzzled as to why the game had stopped. I thought this was hilarious, but I noticed my father and his friends did not appear to agree. Later in the locker room, my father did not spank me. Rather, he yelled at me. Because my father felt more comfortable signing, he often didn't speak. But when he did speak . . . his voice boomed, echoing throughout the lockers.

Towering over me, he had quite an impact. I coiled away with my shoulders up to my ears.

IT WAS NOT FASHIONABLE FOR WOMEN TO WORK in the 1950s. In the 1940s, women had worked outside of the home to support their families while their boyfriends and husbands were in the South Pacific and Europe. But all that changed after the war. Soldiers came home to their families, and a baby boom began. Women had an assignment: Stay home, cook, clean, raise the children. Men had theirs: Bring home a paycheck.

My mother was not that woman. Perhaps my grandmother was her role model, as a schoolteacher. Whatever the factors, all I knew is that because she worked the late shift, she didn't wake up in the morning. After school, I came home and changed clothes and was

From left, my mother Eileen, baby Kyla, my father Melwin, and my son Aaron.

out the door playing with my peers until dinnertime, barely a word to her.

It never occurred to me to feel lonely. This was normal. Every family was like this.

It would take me many years later, beginning in elementary school, to observe that the norm was that fathers worked and mothers stayed home. All I knew was that I saw my mother only on the weekends.

ONE WARM SPRING AFTERNOON when I was thirteen, my father and I had just finished clipping the ivy. We had mowed the front yard, and we were putting the tools back in the garage.

My father signed and spoke simultaneously, asking, *What are you going to do this afternoon?*

I smiled and wiped the stream of sweat from my face. *I am going to play over-the-line, a baseball game with several of my buddies at Pacific Drive Elementary School.*

My father shrugged and with a puzzled look, signed, *I have never heard of the game.* I explained that the game consisted of five players: a shortstop, outfielder, pitcher, catcher, and the batter. Each individual was his own team. The batter batted until he accumulated three outs. Each person had a turn to play a different position and bat. My father smiled and nodded as if to say, "Interesting." Out of curiosity, I signed to my dad, *What sport would you have liked to play professionally?*

He did not hesitate. *Baseball.* He took a batting stance and pretended to hit the ball.

I BECAME THE UNOFFICIAL TEAM MASCOT for the Gold and Green Athletic Association for the Deaf (GGAAD) softball league. I needed to find my niche, and I did. When I was about eight or nine, my father often took me with him to softball games in Los Angeles, where he played in a city softball league. My assigned position was the dugout—so that my dad could keep an eye on me. This ensured that I did not sneak off and cause any disturbances.

As mascot and most ardent fan for my dad's team, I cheered from the sidelines. Like any fanatic, I booed the umpire at any and all signs of injustice. I'd shout, "You blind?" or "Need glasses?" like many other fans. I would get so caught up in the spirit that I did not know my limits. One day, the home plate umpire took offense and stopped the game. I was puzzled. The batter had not been hit by a pitch, nor was anyone running onto the field. The ump called my father over for a chat, and they looked directly at me. My eyes got big, and I had a sinking feeling. This had to be bad.

Together, they strode toward the dugout. I eased quietly toward the bench and sat down. The umpire was big and angry, so I listened intently as he spoke sternly about my offensive screaming and the name-calling. All of a sudden, I was the center of attention: "Get out of the dugout," the umpire bellowed. "You'll sit quietly in the bleachers, and you'll remain there until the end of the game."

In no position to argue, I looked at my father's stern face. He signed, *Listen to the ump.* I got up from the bench, walked slowly out of the dugout, and took my seat in the bleachers. Around me, people nodded and snickered. I assure you I was quiet for the remainder of the game.

AND SO MY CHILDHOOD UNFOLDED, inserting myself between my parents' routines, connecting with my father through sports and mostly passing by my mother on her way out of the house. It never occurred to me to call this loneliness or to think of myself as "on my own" much of the time. This was all I knew.

One morning, while preparing my lunch for school by cutting carrots into strips, the knife slipped, cutting a deep and thick gouge into my left index finger. Without panicking, I calmly grabbed napkins and cleaned the finger as best I could. My mother was still asleep after her night shift, her bedroom closed and curtains drawn. I dashed to the bathroom to find gauze and bandages. *The bleeding will stop,* I told myself. All good. All taken care of. I gathered my lunch and headed out the door and off to school about two blocks away.

Hours later, taking my seat in class, I banged my injured finger on the desk. I screamed in pain. As I examined my finger, I saw blood leaking through, which my teacher noticed, too. Within seconds, too soon for me to hide my finger, she stood over my desk. "You need a nurse," she said.

The nurse's office was a mix of confusion—first sympathy, then anger. "What happened?" she asked as I narrated my very resourceful morning and she cleaned my wound. "Where was your mother?"

5
The Sibs

THE DINNERTIME I knew was like this: my father sat at the head of a long oblong table, my mother to his right. My sister Debbie was positioned on my mother's right with my baby sister Christy between them, and I claimed a place opposite my father at the other end of the table. Another sister, Kathy, sat across from our mom. In their corner, Mom and Dad carried on conversations in sign language. We four kids always had our own animated conversations in spoken language. Occasionally, either Dad or Mom would break in and ask, *What are you talking about?* Debbie or I gave a summary in sign language. Satisfied, they turned back to each other.

Debbie was the good child, the "real" firstborn. Debbie followed the rules, got good grades, went to church, and did all the things our parents wanted her to do. Her arrival, three years after my birth, allowed me to take on the characteristics of the second-born, meaning I was more prone to rebellion rather than being conservative. (However, I do admit I have some firstborn traits: I hate to fail and need to succeed. Things have to be done in an orderly fashion or a certain way. One may even say I am compulsive, or perhaps that is the

Virgo in me.) Throughout our youth, Deb was considered the good seed and I, the black sheep of the family.

Debbie was a tap dancer. When she was about ten, she would come out in a lovely frilly tap-dancing dress and shiny patent leather shoes. She was born in Culver City, California, in late October 1953. When I look at her pictures, she looks like a baby bird to me, tiny and bald. I remember how our mother rubbed Johnson's Baby Oil on her one lock, and combed down the center of her head, a mini-Mohawk of sorts.

INTERPRETING FOR MY PARENTS was the single most frustrating chore I had. By age ten, I had accumulated three younger sisters, which meant babysitting duty, plus I had dishes to do every night after dinner, lawn-mowing and shrub-clipping with my dad, cleaning and sweeping the house, and other chores. Not unusual, perhaps, but the additional task was to interpret, which meant I had to be at their beck and call at all times. Many times, to serve as an interpreter for my parents I had to give up playtime or cancel dates with friends. I often resented these infringements.

Interpreting for my parents was not necessarily a daily event, but it was constant. About once a week, usually on Saturday, while working in the yard, my father would invariably need to borrow tools, like a lawn mower. He would turn to me and tell me what he wanted, and then we would walk next door to ask Mr. Hayes if we could borrow his mower. We usually caught him near the garage near the front porch of his home. Mr. Hayes was a tall, lanky, and very friendly fellow who really liked my parents. My father always stood with me as I asked to borrow the mower. Handing over the mower to my father, both men would smile and my father would, in his voice, thank him and promise to return the mower shortly.

It got more complicated when I had to interpret a doctor's instructions, such as when I was seven and had to interpret how to take the prescribed medicine. Many times, I did not even know what the words meant. For all I knew, I was giving consent for my mother to have a hysterectomy or worse, for my father to have a vasectomy.

Back then, there were no interpreter referral agencies until the 1970s, long after I was out of the house.

For many years we did not have a home phone. My parents obviously did not need one. When people needed to reach us, or we needed to make a call, we went over to our neighbors, the Coates. When people called us, one of the Coates kids came over to give us the phone message, and I went with one of my parents to respond. One day, my father needed to call my optometrist. I dialed the number, and a receptionist answered the phone. I nodded to my father, indicating a person was on the other end of the phone.

I want to make an appointment for David.

I voiced, "I want an appointment for David to see the doctor."

The receptionist gave me a time and date, which I wrote on a piece of paper and gave it to my dad. We ended the conversation, and my father voiced his appreciation to the Coates.

This always felt intrusive to me, using some other family's phone and interrupting their time. Still, they were always nice, and we used the phone sparingly. Even so, this is why when Debbie was old enough, I sloughed off most of my interpreting duties on her. Besides, Debbie was the one who stayed home most of the time while I was out and about with my buddies.

NO ONE EVER GAVE ME AN APPROPRIATE PROTOCOL to interpret for another person. I had to make it up as I went along. All I knew was what had been "justified" by my parents' behavior as acceptable. I would get the information from my parents, and then I would summarize the information to whom my parents would be talking with at the time. In other words, I would get a chunk of information and I would summarize the information, not interpret word for word, and "loosely interpret" in the simplest form that I knew for my age. I was neither eager to master the protocol for interpreters nor to interpret, for that matter. It was not until many years later that, when I started my career at the Arizona School for the Deaf and the Blind, I thought that perhaps I had better learn the professional ethics and etiquette of interpreting.

Years later, when I was thirty-three and just starting my professional career, I was in the teacher's lounge when a woman I'll call Susan, another teacher and colleague who was deaf, asked me to interpret a phone call for her. She emphasized that I was to interpret word for word. I was a bit taken aback. *Word for word?* I signed back.

Susan was visibly upset; that in and of itself was foreboding. I picked up the phone in the lounge and dialed the number Susan gave me. I told her the phone was ringing and then answered by a pleasant voice. She immediately, in a gruff deaf voice and with an angry look on her face on the verge of yelling, signed, *I want to speak to the manager now!*

I voiced her anger with her tone as my face contorted.

The manager got on the phone and asked, "May I help you?" which I immediately signed to Susan.

This is Susan, she signed. *I called before and nothing was done! The service I am receiving at home is shit!* She scowled.

I was a bit uncomfortable at this point, but with my angry voice I repeated to the manager, "The service I am receiving at home is shit!" At this point I told the manager I was the interpreter and I was interpreting for a deaf person on the line.

As the call continued, the manager could not get a word in edgewise. Susan signed, *What the fuck am I to do when you guys never call me back? What kind of damn business do you run?* The words flew off her hands like water out of the faucet. I looked at Susan, hemming and hawing. She gave me a stern look as if to say "Sign what I say." I complied.

The manager remained calm. He told Susan as I signed, *I apologize for the inconvenience. What is your address?* After the call, Susan laid into me *You are my interpreter and I wanted you to sign word for word.*

Yeah, yeah, I know, word for word, I signed sarcastically.

I was angry at the company and wanted them to understand.

I said, *If I had known of the vehemence and anger you wanted interpreted, I would have never agreed to help.* She had put me on the spot. *In the future,* I signed, *I will not interpret for you if I do not know the issue beforehand.*

That was my baptism by fire into the world of interpreting.

MY OTHER SISTER Kathy was the athlete. She arrived when I was seven, and our father attended all of her community softball games.

While Debbie took on the role of interpreter, Kathy took on the role of the quiet one. Debbie became the glue, while I was the adventurer, the one who always tried new things. The dynamics of our family were fully established by the time Kathy came along, with my mother still working the graveyard shift at Hughes Aircraft, my father working at McDowell-Craig, an office furniture manufacturing company. How this dynamic contributed to what would happen later in Kathy's life, I can't say, other than that one of the enduring mysteries in our family was when Kathy disappeared in high school.

If I felt invisible, Kathy may have been more so. My parents did not provide the attention most young teenagers needed from their parents, plus there was the possible negative impact of drugs and ill-chosen friends. All of those were factors in her decision to run away when she was a freshman in high school. I remember my parents were frantic, contacting the police for over two and a half years, and keeping vigilant about whatever clues to the reasons for her disappearance and whereabouts. Rumors flooded in: We heard Kathy was in Gary, Indiana, or maybe another part of Indiana. But all of this came later, when I was out of the house, living at Cowden Hall and working through my freshman year at Northern Arizona University (NAU), working on my own escape.

One cool fall afternoon in 1975, I got a call at my dorm.

"Dave?"

Shivers ran up and down my back. I knew the voice immediately. It was Kathy.

We talked a mile a minute. Kathy was in San Francisco, but our parents didn't know yet. She hadn't had any contact with them for two and a half years.

"Please call them, Kathy," I said, and she promised.

WE WERE NOT a family of money. My mother had been the breadwinner, holding down her night shift job at Hughes Aircraft for twenty-seven years, while throughout most of my childhood, my father worked odd jobs, started a few small businesses, and occasionally worked at Hughes and other companies. Because of this, we struggled periodically.

When my father was out of work, there was only my mom's paycheck to support the family. When I was in elementary school, and Debbie and Kathy were very young, my parents brought home boxes of food and used clothing from the church's welfare store. I was horrified. I really did not mind the food, but the used clothing I refused to wear. My mother tried to convince me that the family had fallen on hard times and that they could not afford new clothing for us kids, but I simply refused to wear other people's clothes. This happened maybe three or four times.

We could count on my mother's paycheck to cover the mortgage, while my father saw to other bills. My father was the "penny pincher," as my mom put it, while she was the person who enjoyed spending the money. My father, however, controlled the purse strings.

When my father worked, we were OK, but again, three or four times, we needed extra help. There was no money for extra things. I never got an allowance. Any pocket money I had, I earned myself by collecting old newspapers, empty aluminum cans, and soda bottles. Luckily for us, California in the 1950s was ahead of its time on environmental issues. I'd cruise the alleys with my dad and Debbie in his old red GMC pickup truck, hoping to make a few dollars from other people's garbage. Often the job was disgusting, as some of the garbage cans were rather stinky. I did not want to share the discoveries with my father and sister; I wanted the treasures for myself. I look back and think about our garage. So many newspapers were stacked in the garage that there was no place for the car. Every other week, we collected enough newspapers for my father to take to the recycle place to exchange for cash. From the deposits we collected we also were able to purchase uniforms for Dad's Gold and Green softball and basketball teams.

My father was talented with his hands. Before I was born, he had started a small office furniture manufacturing business with two hearing partners. His partners took on the business's day-to-day affairs, while my father built large executive desks as well as smaller desks and tables. Dad stayed on as a partner for about four years until we moved to Fullerton.

He also enjoyed building and remodeling homes. One summer, when I was two years old, my dad and some of his friends built an addition to our home in Santa Monica, a house my parents had moved to prior to my birth. Later, when I was eleven years old and visiting my grandparents in Wyoming in the summer of 1962, he decided to do major construction on his parents' kitchen. My grandfather had built my grandparents' home in 1910 and, at the time, it had only one small bedroom, living room, and kitchen. It was, essentially, a log cabin without the logs. If you needed "to go," you had to walk about fifty feet to the outhouse, which was stocked with Montgomery Ward and Sears catalogs instead of toilet paper. When we visited my grandparents during the winter, it was mighty cold without heaters. As their family expanded to seven including my grandparents, the house had not kept up and was in desperate need of a makeover.

My father was just as industrious working around our home, replacing walls, putting in wallboard in the garage, or painting. Over the years, he changed the look of our home. He added office space, enclosed the patio, remodeled and expanded the kitchen, and added a laundry room.

During the mid-1960s, when I was about fourteen, my father began organizing the GGAAD. But one day in the 1970s, my father suffered a spinal injury while moving furniture at an office furniture manufacturing company. A big desk fell on him, making this his last full-time job.

After the spinal injury, which left him with limited ability to work and much more time, my father had further reason to expand GGAAD. I believe this was his delayed dream of coaching baseball. He had turned down an opportunity to become a baseball coach in

Ogden because he wanted to move to LA and start a family. GGAAD was his club and opportunity for him to coach and to realize his long-time dream. My father was very well-known throughout Southern California for his personality, his leadership, his entrepreneurial abilities, his enthusiasm for sports, and his values and convictions for his Mormon faith. He had no problem recruiting young men to play basketball or softball for GGAAD.

THERE WAS NEVER A DULL MOMENT WITH CHRISTY, my third sister, born in September 1960. When Christy was a year old, my parents left me in charge of my sisters and ventured off to a church function. When the time came for me to change her diaper, I placed her on the dining room table and took off her diaper. When I found that I did not have a fresh diaper, I left Christy on the table and went into the bedroom to get one. As I walked back, I heard a thud on the floor and then Christy screaming. Horrified, I started to panic. I picked her up and nervously placed her onto the table to put on her diaper. I really did not understand that she had broken her leg. Luckily my parents soon came home. I tried to explain why my sister was screaming and crying, but no amount of explaining was going to calm them down. They refused to look at me despite my best efforts and focused completely on Christy. Understandably upset, they were not interested in having a conversation with me. I sat at home, devastated, while my parents rushed Christy to the hospital. Today I wonder what they were thinking, leaving an eleven-year-old boy in charge of his baby sister?

As mentioned, my father was Christy's biggest fan. Christy loved to play softball and played throughout school, beginning as a preteen in the Bobby Sox League. But that changed when Christy hit high school. While I was away at college, I worried that my little sister was becoming sexually active too soon. On one visit home, I persuaded her to go to Planned Parenthood. Although she insisted she was not active and the trip was unnecessary, she went. Despite my efforts to head off a crisis, Christy became pregnant at fifteen. My parents were angry and distraught and were concerned about "what people were going to say," how they would look in the eyes of the Mormon Church. They took counsel with the elders in the church. The stake president, the head administrator of a regional cluster of churches, prodded my parents to have Christy give the baby up for adoption to a "good" Mormon family or send her away until after the birth.

I felt that my parents had forgotten about Christy in all their worry and confusion surrounding the pregnancy. It was a Saturday evening about seven o'clock. Summer lingered. The heat of the day was still palpable before the sun set. My father, mother, Christy, and I were in the green room, as we called it, a small room in the back of the house leading to the outside patio. The windows were covered in green fiberglass to provide privacy. As my parents discussed what to do with Christy—throwing around the "possibilities"—I saw the selfishness in them. I saw how they were thinking only about themselves, not about Christy and how this whole pregnancy was playing out in her mind and in her body. She was negligible in the conversation; she sat there, voiceless, listening as Mom and Dad charted out the course of her life and of her unborn child. Words were flying off of their fingers. Tears spilled. I decided to brave it and become her voice. I called for their attention and said, *Christy wants this child. But even more important, she wants and needs your support.* I signed as I spoke, *Let Christy have a say!*

I DO NOT KNOW WHAT WOULD HAVE HAPPENED if I had not been there. Debbie was on her Mormon mission and Kathy, only three years older than Christy, was in San Francisco but had only been in touch with me, so she was not in any position to advocate for her youngest sister. My parents, caught up by the church and its influence, found themselves swayed by the church's interest. I realized that Christy was only fifteen, but ultimately she needed to be the one to make the final determination in her fate. I knew she would never have an abortion. Lost, Mom and Dad handed over their responsibilities to a higher power—which may have been the easy way out.

The year I was twenty-five, still working through college, my little sister Christy, at the age of sixteen, gave birth to my niece, Jessica Eileen Sorensen. They lived with my parents.

THROUGHOUT OUR ADULT YEARS, Christy and I have had a contentious relationship because of our different views toward our parents. Because Christy is a decade younger than me, my relationship with our parents is dramatically different from hers. By the time Christy came around, our folks had been the tried-and-true parents of three children.

When Christy was little, my dad spent more time at home. He ended his role with the LACD and set up his own athletic club, the Gold and Green Athletic Association. By the time Christy was born, my mother worked the day shift and was no longer gone in the evenings. Christy actually had a relationship with our parents—a vastly different connection from what I had growing up. Dad went to her games; he never went to mine. Mom made her breakfast, while Mom had been asleep when I headed off to school.

As adults, when we compared notes, Christy would tell me I tended to be critical of them, how they'd raised us, and how they'd made family decisions. "Look how they responded to your pregnancy!" I would say. "Look how they packed me off to Grandma's when I didn't meet their expectations!" Christy was more guarded; she knew them better.

As each of us has become parents ourselves, we've made our own mistakes. I've learned that children don't come with an instruction manual. There is no proverbial handbook for parents. Funnily enough, Christy and I can debate politics and religion but have to stay well away from the subject of Mom and Dad.

BUT WAIT, THERE WAS TO BE ONE MORE CHILD to fill in our dinner table! Lori was born in December 1963, the last Sorensen baby boomer, so much younger than me that I really did not know her until she was a teenager or even later, when I was living in Oregon and she came to live with me for a while.

With all of the young ones, I did enjoy being the boss. I would tell my younger sisters what to do or not to do. In a way I stayed the oldest, but Debbie and I shared that role. That's because Debbie and I, more than the others, were acculturated into the Deaf community from birth. Cultural mores, characteristics, language, humor, Deaf clubs, academics, residential living, athletics, politics, understanding other disabilities, what cultural minority means and cultural parameters. While my other sisters did learn sign language, their experiences were much different. Kathy was on the tail end of what Deaf culture was all about. By the time Christy and Lori were born and could make some sense of what Deaf culture meant, it was changing so rapidly with communication technology and more community interpreters, and clubs were almost a thing of the past.

MY FATHER'S AND MOTHER'S FAMILIES were similar in regard to their Mormon faith, and both came from farm families. But that is where the similarities end. The distinct differences were in their approach to people.

Grandma Richards, my mother's mother, was very stoic and had difficulty verbally and physically demonstrating love and warmth. It strained her to show affection; when she did manage to hug me, it seemed to cause her physical pain. My mother's hugs were warm, not forced or uncomfortable like my grandmother's. My grandmother was not cold or mean; rather, she was compassionate. Much of her time and money went to her church and school.

One Sunday afternoon when I was sixteen, Grandma Richards and I were sitting in the living room in Joseph City after lunch. She was comfortably situated on the couch, and I eased myself onto a nearby high-back chair. There was a lull as my grandmother leaned over to the left side to pick up a magazine. I was staring out the picture window and occasionally glancing in her direction. I interrupted her reading by gently asking if she missed my grandfather. She turned slowly, and with a soft smile, said, "Yes." Her body language subtly changed. She seemed to transform into another person. She looked at me, but not directly, as if remembering something. I had not seen this soft and gentle side before.

"On Sundays, especially during Sunday school, he had a favorite place to sit in church, near the wall in one of the meeting rooms," she said. "I can often feel his presence." As she spoke, goose bumps prickled my arms. Ten years after he had died, she still remembered him with devotion and love.

On the other hand, my paternal grandparents were always warm, kind, and generous. They gave unconditionally and were very demonstrative in their attention. Hugs, kisses, and gentle talk were the order of the day. As a small child, I felt smothered in love when I was with them. I wiggled in their laps. I wept with laughter as they tickled me. I fell to the ground in horseplay. I felt adored.

However, I can remember when I was about ten years old when my grandmother not so gently scolded Grandpa. As usual, my grandfather had been up at dawn milking the cows in the barn and hand-spreading the feed for the chickens in the coop. Bounding up to the pigpen and looking over the fence, I watched what seemed to be my grandfather wrestling with one of his large hogs, trying to pry something off its hoof. I asked what he was up to. While dancing with a 300-pound hog, he was in no mood to talk. I thought it was funny, but he did not and sent me packing. He hurt my feelings, so I ran to the comfort of my grandmother, crying. After hearing my tale, she went straight from the kitchen to the pigpen and confronted my grandpa. He knew better than to cross her. In the end, without a word to my grandmother, Grandpa made his apologies.

During the summers when I spent time with them on the farm, early morning was my favorite time of day. I always woke up to the smells of my grandmother cooking breakfast and baking sugar cookies. She often took me out to her garden to pick fresh peas and harvest fresh corn. We walked through her orchard to pick the fresh tart green apples and black currants for homemade pie.

As our brief summer vacations came to a close, each of my grandparents took me into separate rooms; first, my grandfather and then my grandmother. Each told me how much they loved me and gave me a warm hug, putting in my hand two or three shiny silver dollars.

MY FATHER WOULD SAY he taught my mother her warmth, although to be fair, over their fifty-two-year marriage, my mother learned to let down her guard. Despite my mother's softening, we were still raised in an atmosphere where affection was rarely displayed between our parents. The times my father demonstrated affection was in a joking manner, smiling and taking my mother into his arms. She'd arch her eyebrow and coyly try to pull away. He'd tell her that he loved her, and she'd blush.

I sometimes wonder what we were learning about marriage on the nights we gathered at the dinner table and had our separate conversations. At the time, I didn't know what it was supposed to look like to have someone to share your day with. We did share our days, but our interactions were limited. The parents spoke to each other while the siblings spoke to each other, both in separate languages.

Among professionals working with deaf people, we talk about incidental learning: what we hear, experience, and glean in our everyday lives. The social interactions and relationships we observe guide us in becoming individuals. When deaf kids grow up in a hearing family, there is very little to glean. A deaf child is not able to hear the verbal interactions between his parents or siblings, especially if they don't sign. If there is fighting, bickering, or abuse, he does not hear it. The deaf child does not hear the verbal scolding or reprimands that his or her siblings incur. In this isolation, the world comes crashing down upon the deaf child when he or she misbehaves and falls on the receiving end of discipline. More times than not, he or she will exclaim, "That's not fair!" "You never punish Jimmy or Susan!" "Why am I getting punished?" Oftentimes the deaf child ends up resenting his siblings as they are the "spoiled ones" while they think, "I am always getting in trouble."

Could this be the same, then, for hearing children raised by deaf parents who lived away from their families? My parents did not have that experience of incidental learning that deaf children get when they live with their hearing families. I wonder now. My parents could have been arguing in sign language in another room of the house, and I would have never known it. Growing up, I saw next to nothing, very little arguing, no discontent or anger toward each other. There were two phrases my parents repeated often. Dad would say, "How would your mother feel?" and Mom would say, "Wait until your father comes home!" I think these two sayings are pretty universal. Can I fault my parents for not being ideal role models for marriage and family? I mean, most of their lives they were brought up in an institutional setting void of much parental modeling of love or providing discipline. They were a product of an era that is difficult to imagine from today's perspective. As a Coda and as a mental health professional who has now worked with hundreds of deaf families over many generations, I see now how much the Deaf culture has evolved. Who or what were my parents' role models? What parent, deaf or hearing, was provided a manual on how to be a parent?

I was born. I had food, shelter, and health care. They provided me with a vast array of experiences: grandparents (four); vacations (Utah, Nevada, Wyoming, and Arizona); a dual culture (deaf–hearing); insights (about minorities and disability); much independence; languages (ASL and English); an athletic body to play different sports; freedom that I can appreciate now, with perspective; their attempt to save my soul (being a Mormon); and to persevere to get what you want. They loved me in their own way despite rarely telling that to my face.

As a child, I did not know I was missing anything. Everything was normal—deaf parents, Deaf culture, and so on. . . . With the perspective of an adult, I understand now something must have been missing, but . . . was there really something missing? There were reasons I did many, many mischievous things (lying or stealing or sneaking out at night or not wanting to go to church or not getting good grades) or positive things (being an athlete). But how was that different from many other children?

I am sure my parents learned as they went along, just as most parents do, including me. I understand more raising my younger daughter than I did with my older son. I had no animosity nor harbor any resentment toward my siblings, nor did I feel left out. I can see my parents learned to be better parents as they matured into parenthood, and things were different for my two youngest siblings. By the time Lori came along, I was thirteen, a handful, and about to become even more of a handful.

6

Breaking the Chains

My mind returns again to those Sunday mornings when our small but growing family made the long trip from Fullerton to Los Angeles to attend church. About an hour after leaving Fullerton, we would finally arrive and park along the tree-lined curb. As we exited the car, we split into two; my father, mother, and baby Debbie would head in one direction to the Deaf Branch while I would walk in the opposite direction.

It was not a long walk. From the sidewalk, I hiked up several concrete steps to the wide walkway to the church building. The church grounds were well-manicured, lined with trees and shrubs. I could see mothers and fathers dropping off their children. Arriving at the doorway, I looked into the long and bright narrow room. Ten wooden pews, sized for us kids, each held seven or eight kids. Several chairs were set out up front for the adults, with a piano to the side. The walls were bright, filled with pictures depicting Jesus or Moses. I took my seat, and we started with a song, my favorite, "Jesus loves me, this I know / For the Bible tells me so. . . ." It was a fun song that I loved to sing.

Year after year, each Sunday our small family of five (and eventually six and seven) piled into the car and made that hour-long trek to Los Angeles. My parents remained faithful to that church, making that thirty-five-mile trip for sixteen years. I look back now and see how hard it must have been to load us up. We were so many moving parts, my sisters and me. But something compelled them to get us all pointed down the road and headed toward our church.

The Mormon community was their anchor, whether at home or school. For my father, Ogden, Utah, was appealing because of its strong Mormon community and that factor was the main reason his parents sent him to the Utah School for the Deaf and the Blind. My mother's parents were also good Mormons, and even though they were far away, they made sure she attended church while she was in school in Tucson. The Mormon faith was really the only thing our parents knew. They wanted the teachings ingrained in us.

The Vermont Ward was the name of a small deaf congregation within a larger hearing community of the Mormon Church in Los Angeles, and my parents were devoted. As the Deaf Branch grew, my parents migrated with it. The Vermont Ward members moved to the Adams Ward, then to Wilshire Ward, all in Los Angeles, where my father was asked to become a counselor or adviser to the branch president, Joe Brandenburg. In 1971, my father was asked to become branch president of a newly built church only for deaf people in Fullerton, where he served until 1988.

While my father was a counselor and later the president of the branch for deaf members, my mother also played a role in the church as a Sunday school teacher. She taught adults the Mormon scriptures. *It is difficult,* she signed to me one day when I was in my twenties. *It is not easy.* Intrigued, I asked why. I watched her hands erupt in a flurry of movement. *Because the Scriptures are complex. The writings are meaningful, but they are hard to interpret,* she said before she rested her hands in her lap.

My mother was used to signing to individuals who had a command of the English language where she did not have to adjust her language register. She signed without concern for the other person's comprehension. She assumed they would understand. Many of the concepts written in the Book of Mormon are very hard to understand even for fluent English speakers. My mother had difficulty bringing her signing to a level of conceptual accuracy to convey the meaning of the subject on which she was lecturing. As I later learned, when I used ASL to teach, I had to define the topic and expand from there. For example, anger: I would have to introduce variables, (e.g., dog, bite, what the person's face looked like). We would then build on these variables (e.g., dog, bite, man, angry face). The dog bite caused the man to have an angry expression. Because of the way ASL is structured, to speak of Mormon concepts, she would have to go build essential concepts to lay the foundation for the Scripture or story being conveyed.

My parents taught me about the Mormon Church not through words, but through the way they lived. They were kind and tolerant. They taught me that racial differences and ability differences were to be viewed through the lens of compassion. They were patient people dedicated to their church.

AT ABOUT TEN YEARS OF AGE, I STOPPED GOING to Los Angeles with the family. I don't think this was about questioning the Mormon doctrines. Rather, my father spoke with Bishop Wilcox in the Fullerton Ward, asking him if I might attend church with his family. My father thought I would get more out of this ward. The bishop said yes, of course, he would be delighted. That meant I no longer went to the Deaf Branch with my own family, and that might have been the beginning of the end of my life as a Mormon. Still, I did attend every Sunday in the Fullerton Ward with the Wilcox family for the next two years. As my family left for church early Sunday mornings, I watched television and got ready for church in Fullerton. The Wilcoxes picked me up, and off to church we went. By the time the Fullerton Ward completed its church services, my parents and siblings were home.

About age twelve or thirteen, I started the Aaronic priesthood and grew more defiant about the church's teachings. The priesthood had three hierarchies: Aaronic, Melchizedek, and Patriarchal. The first level, which I was in, allowed me to participate in ordinances, give service, and help others. We prepared the Sunday sacrament and also once a month made home visits for people in need. At first, I attended the seven a.m. priesthood meetings. The priesthood was an all-male club since women were not allowed to "hold the priesthood." I always thought this was rather odd, but who was I to question the authority at that time?

For about a year, I participated in numerous services that I was permitted to do. At first I attended the priesthood school, but as I became older I questioned the fairness of the church. I met Mormons who smoked and drank. I also did not like the idea of getting up at six o'clock in the morning. All of these things added up, and I began to see how the church was unfair and full of many hypocrites. I saw things at face value that I simply did not agree with.

The priesthood was the start of preparing to go on a Mormon mission. Because of my father's influence in the church, we spent many Sundays entertaining missionaries at our home for lunch or dinner. Looking back, I believe my parents assumed that at age nineteen I would go on the obligatory mission for two years, possibly to Denmark, where my father's ancestors lived and where some of my cousins went. I do not remember any forceful moments growing up that this was mandatory; it was only assumed. To be truthful as I look back, I really never had the aspiration to go on a mission.

Going to church was compulsory. I went because I was afraid of the consequences my father might bring down on me. As a result, he pushed me further and further away. In the end I wanted to make the choice of attending or not attending, and not have someone telling me how religious or spiritual I was to be. To me, this decision is personal and not a group effort.

I did not believe in my father's version of God or religion. Joining an organized religion held as much appeal for me as joining the Elks Lodge or the VFW. I was never much of a joiner. I never had a conflict with religion; as far as I was concerned, it simply did not exist, and how could I have a conflict with something that doesn't exist? I battled with my understanding of spirituality. Believing spirituality could bring serenity, I eventually defined my spirituality with attributes of personal power: humanity, truthfulness, honesty, and integrity.

WHEN SHE WAS NINETEEN YEARS OLD, Debbie went on a Mormon mission to Washington, DC, for two years. She kept in contact with our parents mostly through written communication. Very rarely did she talk with them while on her mission. The church frowned upon any contact between the missionary and her family or relatives, concluding that any contact would distract her from her responsibilities to the church. This sentiment meant that not all family issues were communicated to Debbie while she was gone; my parents censored many details.

Years later on a crisp, wintry evening, I went to visit Deb in Salt Lake City, where she relocated during her twenties. We were chatting about Mormonism and its effect on our family. Deb brought up her feelings of anger and disillusionment toward our parents, one incident being that when Deb had been away on her Mormon mission, Christy had her baby. Upon returning, Debbie had walked into the house to find Christy, living with our parents at the time, holding a baby. Deb was dumbfounded. No one had told her she had a niece. I can only imagine how she must have felt like a complete outsider within her own family. When Debbie disclosed how hurt she had been and how disjointed she had felt from the family, I felt awful and, in retrospect, believe I should have told her instead of assuming she knew. After Debbie returned home from her mission—despite her feelings—she moved back in with our parents and resumed her role as their interpreter.

During her time in Utah, Debbie had become more introspective about her personal values, especially her relationship to the Mormon Church. She told me she felt the church was full of hypocrisy and she was disenchanted with its teachings. She had decided to leave the church.

I had been disenchanted with the church for a long time, just going through the motions through my teens, and was officially out when I became an adult. But her departure from the church threw her into a dilemma that caused her much consternation. She did not know how to break the news to our parents. With great deliberation, she knew she could not face them, so she decided to write a letter outlining her change in ideology, telling them she was resigning from the church. She told me the questions that agonized her: "What will my parents say?" "How will my parents feel?"

"I support what you're doing," I said.

Debbie's revelation devastated our parents. When Debbie returned home from Utah, she was greeted coldly and with indifference. They barely spoke to her. Forgiveness would not be forthcoming until years later.

THROUGH THE YEARS, my parents hosted dozens of missionaries, young people, deaf and hearing, men and women, in our home. All of the missionaries signed. We collected a vast network of family, as many who stayed with us continued to stay in contact. They would call my parents "Mother" and "Father," for my parents had welcomed them with open arms and hearts. I had no problem with this since this was my parents' thing and it was certainly nice. My hospitable parents cared for the young missionaries who came into our home. All being Mormons, they were all on the same page. My father enjoyed youth … basketball, softball, and missionaries. It kept him important and not trivial. It was all reciprocal. His work with missionaries gave him purpose.

But one too many missionaries can crush a family. The Mormon Church was an integral part of my father's life, even too important at times. Hosting missionaries in our home became his supreme focus. If his own children would not remain members of the church, as he had hoped, the parade of missionaries coming through his home was the next best thing. Later, when I was an adult in my mid-twenties and out of the house, my father developed a close bond to one such missionary named Lilly.

Lilly came from a large but poor family in Ireland. Warm and gregarious, Lilly was only twenty-one years old, thin, dark-haired, and petite. Her Mormon faith was strong, and she came to live with my parents. Her mission was based in Southern California. By the time her mission came to an end, she and my father had a strong father-daughter relationship.

When Lilly returned to Ireland, my father, who was in his sixties by then, kept in close contact with her, writing her letters and sending her money. Needless to say, this caused much concern within my family because it seemed very much to my mother and sisters that my father was infatuated with Lilly. My sisters did not address this with my father, but they would meet to discuss the situation and kept me in the loop. My mother was beside herself; she grew very cold to my father, which went on for months and months. My mother was saddened by all the attention my father showered upon Lilly. Her sadness and my father's not recognizing what his behaviors were doing, were what my sisters were most angry about. My sisters and I often talked about this, but we could never confront my father about his behavior. Christy, who was about twenty years old, spent hours consoling my mother and was a great comfort to her as she shared her anger and frustration.

One day, out of the blue, my father sat my mother and sisters down for a conference. He asked the family if we would adopt Lilly. It was clear that a decision was made, unilaterally, that there would be an adoption. Although my mother and sisters were wholly against this, no one dared speak against my father. No one ever thought this could happen, especially since Lilly was in her twenties, so she did not exactly need parents. In the end, none of this transpired. As far as I know, Lilly may not have even known about my father's intention. It was, and still is, my belief that his only purpose in wanting to adopt Lilly was to help her obtain legal status in America. But what disturbed me the most was the approach my father took, going to great lengths to have a daughter in the family who shared his Mormon ideals. He wanted to have a daughter who loved the church as much as he did. He had four daughters, but not one fit his idea of a perfect daughter. By this time, I had completely absolved myself of being a Mormon, and Debbie had told our parents long ago how she felt. So they gave up on the two eldest children ever returning to the flock.

But our departure had opened a gate. By the end of the 1970s, none of my sisters attended the Mormon Church, all of us disengaged.

LOOKING BACK, I see how devoted my parents were to advancing not just the Mormon faith but also advancing it to the community that was the center of their orbit—the Deaf community. The Deaf community was the first, and maybe only, community that understood them. But I didn't always see it that way. For many years, I saw it as a blind faith to Mormonism and as being devoted to anything but us, their hearing children.

That devotion became clear to me years later. Long after I had rejected their faith, they would ask me quietly, "Are you going to church?" They still hoped. I saw how deep their lifelong devotion to the church was when, in 1988, my father stepped down as the president of the branch in Fullerton, and, together with my mother committed to going on a mission to England. Their mission travels took them to Birmingham, Bradford, Manchester, and other places in central England where they were to meet deaf people, educate hearing church leaders about deaf people, and devise a commonality for British Sign Language to communicate concepts of church doctrine. They created signs specific to the Book of Mormon and its doctrine. My parents were the first deaf couple to travel outside the United States for their church and lived in England for eighteen months. By this time, they were sixty-five and fifty-seven years old, and had been married thirty-eight years. *We are sad to leave England,* they told me. *We have met so many nice people.*

IN RETROSPECT, I know my parents struggled to raise five kids and tried to be as successful as they could in all aspects of their lives. They were more successful than most deaf families I knew. Although we were not wealthy, both of my parents had jobs and a nice middle-class home in suburbia. Every year we went on a two-week vacation to visit both sets of grandparents in Wyoming and Arizona. The intangibles such as their faith in their church helped propel their lives. My parents were leaders in their community, and other deaf people would seek my father's guidance in all types of matters, from family and money issues to work and spiritual issues. My father's athletic club helped many deaf people find solace in sports and develop a sense of family and community. During the 1950s and 1960s, many deaf people struggled with money, underemployment, education, and other social issues. This is true even today, but now there are more social networks, support systems, and state and federal laws barring discrimination, as well as community agencies to assist in job training, development, and employment. Though my parents faced challenges in their lives, they were comfortable and thankful for what they had.

7

Breaking Away

FOURTH DOWN, twenty-five-yard line. I said I wanted to kick the field goal. The coach gave me an incredulous look, as did my teammates. But he nodded. My teammates taunted me, and the pressure was on. The center hiked the ball to the quarterback, who placed it on its end in the grass, holding it in place with one finger. I ran to the ball, and with a mighty swing of my leg, kicked it high into the air . . . and through the crossbars. Three points!

Silence. Shock. Everyone froze—the coach, me, my whole team. Then we erupted in cheers. Teammates pounded me on the back as the coach ran onto the field. It was the fall of 1962, and I was new to Nicolas Junior High. But it was clear, with that kick, a kick that no one thought I would ever make, I had hit my stride.

I WAS ESPECIALLY FOND of Coach Davis. He was tall, thin, and athletic-looking. His age, in his late sixties, showed in the weather-worn creases in his face. He sported a flattop haircut, often wearing jeans with a tucked-in shirt bearing the Nicolas Junior High logo, a whistle always hanging around his neck. He spoke in a soft and confident baritone that reflected his warm personality, and he always had a gentle smile. Davis coached many sports, including football, basketball, and track and field. Oddly, he also taught square dancing. It seemed I had known Coach for many years, but I had known him for only a brief moment, one year, during seventh grade. He left a deep impact on my young soul, especially when I needed a father figure.

"Sorensen!" he'd call out when he wanted to give me a kind word or encourage me to work hard at my sport. He taught strategies on how to kick the football or how to stand in the batter's box. I was especially thrilled when he watched the Little League games, where we always acknowledged each other with a smile and a wave. I like to think he attended my games purposely to watch me play, and was sitting in for my dad in a way.

WHEN I RETURNED TO SCHOOL for eighth grade, Coach Davis was nowhere to be found. I was puzzled and asked one of the teachers where he was. "He died over the summer," I was told.

I was devastated. Every part of my body slumped like a rag. I was a very sad eighth-grader. I realized then that I had not known anything about his personal life. I did not even know if he was married, had a family, or had grandkids. This was the first time someone I cared for had died, and it was a new experience. I continued to play Little League, but I felt something was missing: his watchful eyes at my games.

ALL THROUGH ELEMENTARY AND JUNIOR HIGH, I lagged behind academically. I barely passed with Cs and Ds. By the time I got to Sunny Hills High School, I was struggling to fit in. I had few friends there because most of my buddies went to other high schools.

One day in math class, I was cutting up, and Mr. B directed me to stay after. I had no intention of doing any such thing. Mr. B was no taller than I and nowhere near as muscular—rather wimpy, some would say. My plan was to simply drift out the door.

When he grabbed my arm, I was taken aback. I shoved him hard and fled. A classmate witnessed the incident and made a joke at Mr. B's expense. I bragged that it was no big deal. The following day, I discovered what a big deal it really was. I was suspended from school for several days. My father was furious.

To get back into school, my father and I had to attend a meeting with Mr. Robertson, the assistant principal, a large man with a big head full of short, coiffed brown curls. I thought I might be doomed, but no interpreter was available, which meant I would be the interpreter.

When Mr. Robertson spoke, I signed exactly what I wanted my father to know. I did not change the principal's words, but I did minimize what he was saying. I conveyed the content, but changed ever so slightly the significance of the words.

When Mr. Robertson said, "David hit Mr. B," I signed, *Pushed.*

I knew my father could read lips pretty well, but I got away with it. As we went to leave the principal's office, I thought my father seemed supportive of me. "You should not have done that," my father spoke. "You could have done something different."

It was not a long and angry diatribe. Walking out, my fait accompli had been easy. My father had blamed Mr. B for manhandling me in the first place, and so his frustration with me dissolved. I was happy to accept my punishment: Reassignment to another math teacher for the rest of the year. I remained gleeful about my cunning interpreting skills.

FOOTBALL MAY HAVE SAVED ME from worse incidents. The fall of my freshman year, I practiced every day after school. The workouts and drills were long and strenuous. As a fourteen-year-old, I was rather lanky at five foot nine inches and 140 pounds. I enjoyed running, which benefitted me because most of our practice time was spent building endurance, including wind sprints and longer and strenuous runs up and down the hillsides near the practice field. The cardio part of practice I found simply tiresome, but I kept with it.

I sensed that one of my new football coaches liked me. He spent much of his time hounding me through the drills. I felt like I was in basic training enduring drill sergeants screaming, yelling, and spitting in my face; I felt loved. The coach barked out encouragement: "Keep running! Slow down! Run faster! Run harder!" Finally, someone was paying attention to me. I practiced during the end of the summer into fall, but despite the coach's encouragement and my initial excitement, my commitment to football waned. Not that I did not like football; I just wanted to do something different. I fell into a pattern of trying sports—football, water polo, basketball—and then quitting before the season ended.

I did some really crazy things when I was in high school. On my way home during my freshman year I decided to stop off at the Village Market, a small neighborhood store. As I walked into the store, my eyes scanned for the candy section. I walked over to the display case and checked out the various candies. One problem: I did not have any money with me. I looked around to see if anyone was in the vicinity, and it was all clear. I picked up a Baby Ruth bar and stashed it into my pocket. I turned around and headed out the door.

The cashier grabbed my shoulder. "Did you take something?"

"No," I said.

"What do you have in your pocket?"

My stomach sank. The man guided me over to a chair near the counter and told me to sit down. He did not say a word as he picked up the phone. I did not hear the conversation, but I knew he was not calling my parents.

Ten minutes later a police officer drove up to the front of the market. The cashier motioned him in, and they spoke briefly. The officer signaled me over.

"Did you steal the candy bar?" the officer said.

I admitted to the crime.

"Never return to this store," the cashier said as I exited with the police officer.

I did not say a word as I followed the officer to his car. He opened the front door on the passenger side. I crawled into the seat as the officer walked around the car, opened the door and situated himself in the driver's seat.

"What is your parents' phone number?" he said.

By this time, my parents did have a phone. I quickly responded to his request, and he wrote it down on a piece of paper. He then started the engine and drove off from the store. We arrived at the police station and walked into the main lobby where I sat for a few minutes. Soon, another officer escorted me through a door that led down a long corridor. The officer inserted a key into the lock, turned the key and opened the door. His eyes met mine. "This is where you will be staying until your parents come to pick you up."

A few hours later, from my jail cell, I heard noises out in the hallway. I stood on my tip-toes to peer through the bars. A whole classroom of junior high students was coming through for a tour. And today they would get to see a real criminal. I quickly sat back down on the bed. Kids came up to my cell and peered in at me. "Why are you in here?" "What did you do?" One boy remarked, "Oh, cool."

The police had a hard time trying to contact my parents. They had to wait until my sister came home from school. After my mother got the news, she decided to wait until my dad got home before they collected me. A few hours later, I heard the door open again down the hallway. Footsteps approached my cell, and an officer unlocked my cell. "Follow me," he said.

My parents stood at the officer's table. They did not seem angry. My mother did not say much. It was my dad. He immediately took charge. "Why did you do that?" he spoke with his voice. "You should not have done that!" Everyone around could hear his displeasure with me. He wanted to make sure I was listening and so he used his voice. If I had been deaf, it would have been different. I could have easily blown him off by turning my head and not paying attention to him.

But no, I had to hear it.

ANOTHER TIME, MY BUDDY ERIC and I hatched a plan to meet up later in the evening to hang out and talk as we walked the neighborhood. Eric lived only a few blocks from our house. Our plan was all innocent, nothing insidious.

We were to meet on the corner of West Avenue and Basque at eleven o'clock. That was the perfect time because my father would be in bed after watching the news. When I did not hear any more movement from my father in his room, I knew the coast was clear. I got up and dressed in Levi's jeans and a t-shirt. I went out the front door and walked to our designated meeting place. It was a warm night in early spring. I met Eric, and all we did for an hour or so was walk and talk before we decided to go home.

I am pretty sure Eric's walk home was not as eventful as mine. I suddenly noticed car lights shining on my back. *It can't be the cops,* I told myself, but the lights approached and soon a car came alongside me. Police.

"You got an ID?" the officer said.

"Just out for a walk, sir," I said. "I'm heading home."

I guess he did not believe me. "In the car," he said, motioning.

He opened up the back passenger door and I got in. He got into the car, put it in gear, and we drove to the police station. The officer escorted me into the station and asked me to sit in the lobby where the officers could observe me. The officer asked me for my parents' phone number, which I provided.

Sitting there, I pictured the ringing phone, my sister Debbie answering, walking from the living room to the hallway, craning her head around the door to my parents' room. She would turn on the hall light and walk in, where my dad would be sleeping on the side of the bed near the window. She would shake him gently. At first he would be groggy, then more alert, then upset. I checked the clock. It was almost midnight, and my mother was still at work. She would not get home until 1:30 a.m.

At the station, my father told the officers he was deaf. I watched the officers attempt to talk with him awkwardly. My father pulled out paper and started to write out what he wanted to say. I watched my father's face, which had a look of frustration as he peered over at me sitting across the room. We left the police station and drove home. My father pointed out that this was the second time he had to pick me up from jail.

FOOTBALL BROUGHT HIGH HOPES. Perhaps if I were on the football team, I could attract attention from the girls. I needed as much help as

I could get. I was not the most handsome guy around. Although tall and of average weight, I had geeky hair and was pimple-faced. Because my father had been the appointed hair cutter when he had boarded at the deaf school in Utah, I guess he thought he was hot stuff and could save a few bucks by cutting my hair. I dreaded my haircuts because I looked as though someone had put a bowl on my head and shaved around it. Not a good look for a teenager trying to impress the chicks.

Regardless of the pimples and wretched hair, I did manage to find a short-term girlfriend, Claudia. She was very short, with a round body and brown shoulder-length hair. I did not care what she looked like as long as she liked me; I was desperate. My friend Eric introduced us, and she lived in Brea, the next town.

Claudia was my first true love. She called me and we made arrangements to meet on Valencia in front of my old elementary school, Pacific Drive. We walked around the school holding hands. We sat down on one of the school benches, and it was there Claudia christened my lips with my first kiss. What a kiss it was. I wanted our lips to be joined forever. The day after that indelible kiss, I saw her for the last time, since I left for Arizona for the summer.

I WAS PETRIFIED of my father. He was a big man; I was a skinny kid. Sometimes he would come after me with his long, thick leather cowboy belt, the one with his name embossed on the back. He would lash it into me so hard that it left an imprint of his name on my hindquarters. He would yell in a booming baritone. Other times, he spoke to me in a calm, resigned voice. The truth was, I was afraid of him because I never knew how he would react.

My fear didn't stop me from trying to get away with things. One night my friend Eric and I planned to sneak out of our houses sometime after nine o'clock. I didn't have my own bedroom, though. I slept in the den on a rollout couch, and I always kept the door closed because my father watched television in the adjacent living room. It might have made more sense to slip out at eleven o'clock after my dad went to bed, but Eric and I had a plan.

That night, I pretended to get ready for bed. With most of the house settled, I said goodnight to my father. I peered through the crack of the sliding pocket doors to be sure he was in his easy chair. I then grabbed my pillows and a blanket so I could fashion what resembled a sleeping body underneath the covers. I walked over to the window, opened it, and slipped out, leaving the window ajar to get back in later.

We had no particular plan. We walked the streets at night. Eric, who was a year older, was short and stocky with brown hair cut in a surfer style with long bangs, hair hanging to his shoulders. After a couple of hours, we said our goodbyes. I returned to my bedroom window only to discover that the window was closed. The door to the den was open and the blankets and sheets drawn back.

Beyond the door, I could see my father sitting in his easy chair, television still on. Oh, shit, now what am I to do? I thought. You could say I was a bit panicky. All I could think was, "I'm going to get the hell beat out of me." Even though my father never used his fists, I was more afraid of his screaming.

I walked around the house and opened the side door to the laundry room. It was now around eleven-thirty or midnight, and I knew my mother would be home in fewer than two hours. I remained in the laundry room until my mother came home; I did not want to attempt going to my room because I would have had to pass my father watching television. My heart pounded as I pondered all sorts of terrible impending punishments. Waiting for my mom was terrifying, but somehow I thought she would save me. So I waited.

At last, I heard her footsteps in the kitchen. I moved to hide behind a cupboard, then I heard her step down into the laundry room. She turned on the light. *David, what are you doing?*

I snuck out of the house, I signed to her. *I was scared to face Dad, so I hid in here.*

Slinking behind her, I walked with her out of the laundry room, through the kitchen, and into the living room where my father sat. In my mind, all I could see was this tall man screaming at me as I sobbed. All my fears melted away as my father and mother began to sign to me. *Why did you sneak out?* my father asked calmly.

As Mom watched, I said, *I wanted to hang out with a friend.* Both sat patiently, looking at my face. I again waited to see the anger surface on my father's face. *I was afraid to ask for permission,* I signed.

My parents looked at each other, and without a word my father nodded his head, motioning me toward the den. Go to bed, he was telling me. My punishment was my fear of being punished.

WHILE I WAS GRAPPLING with the garden-variety adolescent struggles of pranks and girls and football, my father had his mind on something else entirely. He worked during the day, immersed himself in Mormon activities on the weekends, attended sporting events, or watched television. I can see him now, in his pajamas, reclined in his easy chair with a sixteen-ounce glass bottle of RC Cola, his Planters Peanuts floating on top. I don't think I was on his radar screen at all.

In June 1965, I was fourteen years old. It was the summer my parents planned to attend the Deaflympics on the East Coast. My parents were excited—especially my father, who wanted to champion his players. He recruited several players from the Gold and Green Athletic Association for the Deaf to compete in swimming, ping pong, and the javelin. The Deaflympics occur every four years, just like the hearing Olympics. They are hosted by competing international cities and showcase the best deaf and hard of hearing athletes in the world. My parents took two weeks off work so they could attend. While they were gone we stayed with my grandmother in Arizona. I was handed the responsibility of supervising my younger sisters Debbie, Kathy, and Christy while they were away. Lori, who was only two years old, went with my parents to the East Coast.

This was freedom!

Every day in Joseph City, I could hang out with my cousins and meet new friends. My parents were not gone for more than a few days when I tapped Debbie to watch Kathy and Christy so I could take off with a cousin on an adventure of undetermined nature.

Debbie was not thrilled, but complied.

My cousin Richie and I took off in his family truck, a rugged blue 1956 Chevrolet that had seen better days. We headed south of Joseph City on a dirt road about ten miles out. Coming to a flat piece of land, my cousin decided to make doughnuts, driving in tight circles at high speeds. What a thrill it was kicking up a tornado of swirling dust that could be seen for miles. As we drove back to town, my cousin hit a dirt curb and lost control of the truck. We flipped over twice and everything went into slow motion. It took a few minutes to come to a complete stop. I was ejected from the truck and the old Chevy landed on top of me. As I tried to gather my bearings, I noticed an arm splayed in an awkward position to my side. I thought it was Richie's. Just then, Richie picked up the side of the truck and heaved it upright. The arm was mine. I figured I'd fractured the upper arm, and I panicked. What the hell were we going to do now? I rose slowly, keeping my arm in an "L" position against my stomach. Terrified, we were about five miles from town. Several cars and trucks slowed down, but we waved them on. I was petrified that I might lose my arm, and could see my dreams of playing basketball disappear. We finally made the long walk back to Richie's house, and he called his father. My uncle was calm as he drove me to the hospital in Holbrook, about ten miles east. I was admitted for two days. They released me a little bruised and battered, with my arm in a sling. I felt like a bird that had broken its wing. But my arm healed and my hysteria passed with the summer. My grandmother had to wait to inform my parents about my accident. She did not know where they were staying or how to call them.

A broken arm was not going to stop me from having one of the best summers of my life. The summer quickly filled with church activities and afternoons at Cholla Lake. The lake was close enough that we could either walk or ride our bikes. I hung out with my cousin Kelsey, who was born on the same day I was. He was not too tall, and rather thin, sporting short brown hair and a caustic sense of humor. Kelsey's father owned a motel and gas station, and I lolled about the gas station, swapping stories with Kelsey and my uncle, having a laugh. Sometimes I pumped gas, checked oil, and washed windows for customers.

Across the street was the Pacific Café, where all the kids hung out. The Pacific reminded me of the diner from *Happy Days.* There was the blasting jukebox and two pool tables in the back. I thought this was paradise. These were my happy days; I was popular and living it up. In this tight-knit community, everybody knew each other.

By the first of July I knew my parents would be returning soon to Joseph City from their Deaflympics trip and find out about my misadventure with my cousin. I knew my father was not going to be pleased: I had neglected my responsibilities to my sisters and had broken my arm in a reckless accident. Dread crept into my easy days. By the time they finally arrived, I was miserable. As expected, my father screamed at me. "You cause all sorts of problems for everybody!" After a few days, Dad cooled off. I'd punished myself: I was the one with a useless, bound-up arm that would take a couple of months to heal.

During the previous school year, I had smoked cigarettes, shoplifted at the Rexall drugstore, and stolen money out of my mother's purse. I lied to people about anything, never discriminating to whom I lied or about what I was lying. In truth, I was desperately seeking my father's attention. I felt I had legitimately pursued his approval by excelling in sports, but to no avail. He rarely attended my games and was stingy with his encouragement. I felt invisible, and this was my way of lashing out. My grades in ninth grade were in the low Cs and Ds. The truck incident was the last straw for my parents. As this list of offenses rolled out, I did not have a clue that my parents were talking with my grandmother about my future. It came as a surprise to me, albeit positive, that I was to stay and attend high school in Joseph City.

As my parents prepared to return to Fullerton, they conferred with Grandma Richards and cemented the plan to leave me behind. The plan was open-ended. I would attend Joseph City High School, maybe for a year, or maybe I'd stay through graduation. I loved the idea of living in Arizona. For my parents, it was out of desperation in hopes I would change my ways. In any event, I'd been welcomed into embracing arms. I'd made new friends and was loving life. I was a big fish in a small pond. I was the big-city boy. My friends called me the "California Surfer." I looked the part, constantly flipping my long sandy blond hair out of my face. I was cool.

At the time I really didn't explore why my parents handed me over to Grandma. Not until years later, while working through issues with a counselor, did I even consider that my stay in Joseph City was not about me, but rather about my parents and their inability to cope with me. I later came to suspect that they relinquished their responsibility of me because they hoped that a change of venue and friends would shake me free from my wild behavior. Perhaps they'd hoped I'd turn my grades around, attend church, and be more honest and responsible. Nobody ever discussed the reasons with me. It could even have been simply that my parents felt ill-equipped to raise me.

PART THREE
Soul Searching

8
Quiet Anger

After my parents decided to leave me in Arizona, I settled into a new normal. Mostly, I was having a blast with my new freedom, and somehow, this allowed me to do well in school. As an adult, I now understand what was missing, how this set a new dynamic in motion in our family, creating challenges that I would have to bridge later in life.

While in Arizona, I thought of my sisters often. I still do; I truly loved them. I am pleasantly surprised in adulthood to discover that despite the fact that I was never really around as a big brother, we have settled into close relationships as adults. We've become friends. When I'd left home at age fourteen, my sisters were eleven, seven, four, and two. Sure, I'd babysit them if my parents went out, but carelessly. Mainly, I paid them little heed. If I were home in California during the Christmas holidays or summer, I would scurry away from them, opting to pal about with my friends or heading off to the beach. I've been a bit sad that I didn't grow up with my sisters, that we weren't thick as thieves, that I hadn't been given their secrets to keep, and that I wasn't their friend.

During high school, I lived much like my parents had while they were at boarding school. Like them, I too visited home occasionally rather than living there full-time. Often I felt like a stranger in my own home. Little sisters would be scattered at my feet, as unrecognizing of me as I of them. It seemed each time I visited home I was trying to reestablish ties; each time I came home I had to start over. To them, I was just the brother who lived in Arizona.

My father started school in Utah in the early 1930s, while my mom began her education in Tucson in the latter part of the 1930s. Residential schools for deaf students today are much different than they were back then. Dorm parents were much older, and teachers and staff members then tended to be paternal. Most of the female staff members were postmenopausal and old-fashioned. They pulled their hair back in tight buns and wore dresses that cut off midway between their knees and ankles, and plain black shoes with clunky heels. The way they spoke was direct and straightforward, incorporating an almost militaristic discipline. I am not suggesting that young deaf kids were subject to cruelty; rather, the adults around them operated in a manner different from today. No married couples supervised students in the dorms, so those kids did not see very many happy marriages, or perhaps even see marriages at all. Most staff members could not sign or communicate with the students, which seems astounding to think about now. The dominant philosophy then was an emphasis on oral communication, stressing that deaf people had to learn to assimilate into the larger society, and this could be done by learning to speak. But the deaf children usually went undercover, learning to sign among themselves during recess, in the dorms, and outside of the classroom.

To say the least, staff members at the boarding schools were no substitute for parents. So you can imagine that if these students were not able to communicate or convey their basic needs to the staff, they certainly could not express that they missed their parents. The school provided food and shelter, but that was about it. Many of the students lived 100 or 200 miles from home, and back then, transportation was a challenge. For those whose parents lived in extreme rural areas, communication with their parents simply didn't happen.

Today, in the more contemporary residential schools, it is a much different environment. There is a mix of young adult staff members who are barely older than some of the high school students they supervise and older staff members. They dress more casually, and they are encouraged to build relationships with their charges. More deaf staff members live in the dorms. More teachers are deaf or can sign. Communication thrives. Visits with families are more frequent because of the ease of transportation, usually going home every weekend. Thanks to advanced technologies such as video relay services, FaceTime, Skype, videophones, and iPhones, contact with their parents flourishes.

In either case, though, there *is* a sense of family, a deaf family. Many of the kids who attend residential schools live together for ten to fifteen years, creating lifelong bonds as they naturally adopt each other as surrogate brothers and sisters. Oftentimes, these bonds are stronger than the bonds they form with their own biological families. Back then and today, it is not unusual that as kids grow older, they prefer to remain at school or stay with friends during the holidays rather than return home. For too many deaf children, home is a place of noncommunication, a place of boredom, or even a place of isolation.

YEARS LATER, AS A YOUNG ADULT in my twenties, during a counseling session with my therapist, my anger, or rather disappointment, spilled over toward my mother, for not being available, toward my father for not understanding, and toward myself for being born to deaf parents. This session was while I was attending NAU with a counselor working a psychology internship at the university counseling center.

The counselor and I touched on the topic of my parents being deaf. Most every hearing person is fascinated about the deaf part of the family when I talk about my background, and this session was no exception. When I spoke, I was not frothing at the mouth, yelling and screaming. Rather, I was reflective, using a soft voice. I told the counselor I had never felt anger that my parents were deaf, nor had I ever thought that I did not want deaf parents. It had been long ago settled in my mind as a matter of fact that I had deaf parents. I thought that was just normal. My belief was that parents, deaf or not, needed to value their children and pay attention to them.

In that session, I came to see this belief was a double-sided coin. Sometimes I was the "good kid" through athletics. If that didn't get their attention, I would be the "bad kid," always vying for attention by lying or stealing or general shenanigans. It was not passive, but indirect. I never said to my parents point blank, "You were lousy parents because you never did this or you never did that." But I *was* saying it. I was saying it through my behavior.

JOSEPH CITY WAS A SMALL FARMING COMMUNITY of about 500 people. The town was divided in half by Route 66. Each side of the road was lined thickly by old, majestic cottonwood trees, giving the impression that you were driving through a tunnel. Agricultural ditches ran alongside, providing water for the townspeople's gardens and lawns.

The high school was small, which meant we could do many more things than some of the larger ones. We did not have any choice in curriculum; we shared the same schedules and classes. We could join band and varsity sports, including flag football, basketball, and baseball. We were a tight class, and in fact, many of us were related. We had sock hops after our basketball and baseball games. Almost every person who lived in town attended our school sporting events. My prowess on the sports field earned me a great deal of attention. I was a starter on both the basketball and baseball teams, and that meant field trips around the state.

The sophomore class trip to Phoenix was a big deal. The day we left, we piled into a small yellow school bus. The morning was a bit cloudy, but as we headed west toward Flagstaff, the clouds thickened and rain changed to snow. As we made our way into Phoenix, it transitioned to rain again. Our bus pulled into the Kon Tiki Hotel, our home for the next few days. After stashing our things in our rooms, we made a beeline for the swimming pool, oblivious of the rain still pouring from the sky. People must have thought we were insane, but the mid-sixties temperatures seemed balmy after the chills of Joseph City. In the next few days we toured Arizona's largest newspaper, *The Arizona Republic*, and saw the musical *The Sound of Music*. The trip solidified the intimacy of our class. And we returned home abuzz.

My extracurricular activities kept me busy and maybe even *in* trouble. In the evenings I'd often be at the Pacific Café helping the Hancock family, who owned the restaurant, cooking, serving, or pearl diving (washing dishes). I filled my weekends with camping, hunting for rabbits, and jumping into my friend's sand buggy in the badlands. I also met my obligations of attending Priesthood, an all-male fraternity in the Mormon Church, Sunday school, and Mutual, a church youth group held every Tuesday evening.

Moving from California to Arizona did not change me or fix me as perhaps my parents had hoped. I met Jack, Dick, and Johnny, and we'd raise hell. We got a reputation. If something was found broken or went missing, we were the ones to blame. On the nights of Mutual we'd arrive late after cruising the streets, playing pool at the café, and smoking cigarettes. We'd saunter down the aisle as people spun around to watch us skulk in. You could hear them say, "Hmmm, they smell like smoke." We'd pick a pew and slouch against each other. We were nicknamed the "Joseph City Mafia." But in truth, we were not quite so glamorous. We were not assassins or extortionists, nor did we run cathouses or deal drugs. We were just a gang of kids who drank and smoked. We had, on occasion, stolen meat from our uncles' houses to eat and, with BB guns, we'd shoot out the lightbulbs of the street lamps. We were fairly cooperative during the day and found courage for antics in the shadow of night.

Although my buddies knew my parents were deaf, it seldom surfaced as a topic for conversation. However, what did catch their interest was signing, something they were eager to learn. I taught them how to fingerspell since they figured that fingerspelling would come in handy especially during quizzes. In Mr. Hansen's biology class, we gave each other the answers to the multiple-choice and true-false portions of the test. Our little tricks died a quick death when Mr. Hansen caught on. He bawled us out for cheating and separated us for the remainder of the test. After class, Mr. Hansen's good-natured demeanor returned, and somehow I knew he had found some humor in the prank.

The summer between my sophomore and junior year, my parents and sisters made their only trip to Joseph City while I was living with my grandmother. One afternoon my buddies and I ventured out to the badlands for a drive. We invited my father to go with us, which he did. I decided to have a little fun on my friends' account. I was sitting shotgun, Dick was driving, and my father was sitting in back with Jack. I started into a tirade using four-letter expletives: "f" this and "h" that and "s" this. I was laughing my head off while my buddies panicked—their mouths dropped open, their eyes widened. I was hilarious. They thought I'd lost my mind until I said, "My father is deaf, guys. He can't hear me."

JUNIOR YEAR BROUGHT CHANGE. My class transferred to Holbrook High School, where the student body was about 600 students, compared to only sixteen students in my sophomore class at Joseph City. At seven o'clock each morning, Monday through Friday, the Joe City bunch, as the students in Holbrook called us, met at the high school bus barn in Joseph City. Uncle Keate, my grandmother's brother, drove us into Holbrook. We were not the most quiet and respectful of teenagers. We got up from our seats and tossed spit wads at each other. Many times Uncle Keate had to pull the bus over to the side of the road and lecture us. He lasted only a year.

Holbrook High School was vast. I preferred the familiarity and closeness of our small class at Joseph City and found myself disoriented transitioning into the new school. My grades plummeted abruptly. Competition in sports was fierce. I managed to make the junior varsity football team as an official bench warmer, and I lasted until the first snowstorm. As I sat there fuming, freezing my butt off on the sidelines, I lost my patience. Coach was barking at me that warming the bench for the other players was my job. By the end of the week, I quit. I was encouraged to play baseball, at which I excelled, but my interest waned; it was more fun to party than to play ball.

By the time I came home for Christmas vacation during my junior year in 1966, a cultural revolution had ushered in a new era. The war in Vietnam was killing our young men unjustly; it was the era of love-ins, peace-ins, and flower power. Universities and colleges were besieged by riots and peace marches. This was the era of free love and drug experimentation. Music changed the lives of young people. It was a time of reflection. It was the time of the Beatles, and I was in the middle of it all.

I smoked pot for the first time when I was home to see my parents for Christmas. My friend Randy and I were hanging out, and decided to amble over to the local Alpha Beta supermarket early in the afternoon. Standing between cars in the parking lot, Randy offered me what looked like a rolled cigarette. "Marijuana," he said. At first I hesitated, but I knew I'd give it a try. He lit the joint and took a deep breath before he offered it to me. No stranger to smoking, I placed the joint between my lips and took a long drag. Randy instructed me to hold in the smoke before I exhaled. We passed the joint between us until it was gone. I felt lightheaded, and everything around me—cars and people—moved slowly. My body felt as if it was gliding as I walked. When I spoke it was deliberate and methodical. I was high for nearly three hours. When I went home, although high, I acted normally. I did not think my parents knew I was stoned, especially since pot was a relatively new phenomenon.

My final year of high school rolled along much as my junior year. I had no interest in academics and did not plan on attending college after graduation. I had no plans whatsoever. My interest in school was purely social; I attended classes solely to be with my friends. Even so, I missed more than seventy days of school. On those days I wandered the eleven miles of railroad track back to Joseph City, feeling like Huck Finn.

On one of my treks home on the railroad tracks, I noticed in the far distance, through the tamaracks and bushes, what appeared to be a rundown homestead with only a skeletal frame remaining. I doubted anyone had lived there in over thirty years. Nearby was the main house, which too had fallen into decay. After treading carefully into the house, I made my way to the living room. The floors were made of wooden planks and everything was coated with dust that had blown in through the open doors and broken windows. There were remnants of furniture. I could see from the living room two bedrooms, a small kitchen, and bathroom.

As I began to poke around, I came across a walk-in closet in one of the bedrooms. There wasn't much to see, but as I turned away I caught a glimpse of what seemed to be a stack of magazines high up on a shelf in the back of the wardrobe. I reached up tentatively, envisioning my fingers stumbling into a brown recluse spider or scorpion. What I found were backdated issues of *Life* magazine as well as old issues of the local *Holbrook Tribune* from the early 1930s. As I read through the newspaper, I was shocked to find myself reading about Grandfather Richards. He'd been involved in an auto accident. After spending more time than I should have, I took the newspaper and headed west along the tracks toward home.

Back in Joe City, I walked into my grandmother's house to find her preparing the evening meal. I helped set the table, placing silverware, condiments, and napkins. We made our usual small talk, asking each other about the day. I of course did not mention my field trip to the abandoned farmhouse. I did, however, ask her about Grandpa and his car accident. She looked up at me with surprise as one of her eyebrows shot up, saying, "What?" I told her a made-up story that led to my finding an old edition of the *Holbrook Tribune* and coming across the article about Grandfather Richards. She shook her head and told me that she had long forgotten about that accident. My grandmother: a woman of few words.

ONE TEACHER IN PARTICULAR validated my truancy. Picture this: Thirty students lined up in rows facing the front of the class. My US history teacher sits at his desk at the rear of the class. His lecture begins, "Turn to chapter seven, page 113." When we find the selection, he reads each and every word from the book and we, dutiful students, follow each and every word, with the exception of a handful of students who are astute enough to fall asleep. We were bored out of our minds. How was I expected to put up with this nonsense?

If it was not for my favorite teacher, Jim Reese—the typing teacher and Holbrook High School's varsity baseball coach—I would not have graduated that year. Mr. Reese wasn't going to let me fail. Knowing that I needed to pass Mr. Munoz's bookkeeping class, Mr. Reese intervened and negotiated a deal with Mr. Munoz: If I could manage to get a C on the final exam, he would give me the credit I needed to graduate. I passed the class and subsequently graduated—third from the bottom. In retrospect, if I had not managed to graduate, I probably would have dropped out for a while. I just couldn't tolerate another US history class.

One morning during my senior year I was sleeping on the foldout couch in the front room. My grandmother was struggling to get me up for school. I knew she was getting frustrated with me, but I was getting annoyed as well. I told her I did not want to go to school. There was no reason; I just did not want to go. I crossed the line by calling her a bitch. She snapped, "Get up and get out!" I hurriedly complied, throwing on my clothes, skipping breakfast, and heading down the driveway. I made my way toward the bus barn to catch the bus to Holbrook.

During the day I told my buddy Jack about what I had done that morning. "I'm not going to stay with her anymore," I said. We considered my options. I decided to make my new home in the abandoned Pacific Motel. It had been boarded up for many years and served as only a warehouse for my uncle. Route 66 no longer bisected Joseph City. Along with the Pacific Motel there were gas stations and trading posts that also lost the tourism travel. The new highway, Interstate 40, had been built a quarter-mile south of town, which diverted the tourists who had once poured dollars into our small community. The motel sat on the northeast corner of Route 66 and Bushman Road. The Mormon Church was across the street and Midway Dairy was next door to the east. In the front, where the guests checked in, was the gas station. The motel had fourteen small units laid out in the shape of a U. I chose a room in the back corner of the motel. I used the back alley to come and go undetected. The afternoon I moved in, some friends and I pried open a window and slipped in. We cleaned up the room as best as we could. Later Jack would bring sleeping items, food, and candles.

I managed to take showers at my grandmother's home while she worked or ran errands. Jack or another buddy washed my clothes at their houses. After three days, Jack persuaded me to stay with his family. I knew he had talked with his parents to get their permission. I was hesitant, but not stupid; I accepted the offer. Jack's parents did not pressure me, nor did they ask a lot of questions, although they did encourage me to speak with my grandmother. I loved Jack's family and appreciated everything they did for me. Jack's father worked at the local power plant, and the meager income he brought home was stretched thin raising four boys. I lived with them the last three months of my senior year. They made me feel like their fifth son.

During that time I did not miss a day of school. A couple of times my grandmother came over to Jack's to try to persuade me to return home. She was stern, and I was stubborn. I said I didn't want to come home, that the idea of it made me feel uncomfortable. I did apologize for calling her a bitch, and beneath her stoic exterior I saw the smile anyone else would have missed. I held no animosity toward my grandmother; I just had no inclination to return.

Knowing that my parents were coming, I moved back to my grandma's house the week before graduation. I did not want them to know that I had moved out. Although I was fairly sure my grandmother had shared with them what had transpired during the past months, none of us said a word.

The day I graduated from Holbrook High School in May 1968 was a marvelous day. After three years living away from my parents, after a long stretch of my reckless disregard for all institutions of learning, I had received a high school degree. I had earned the rite of passage to enter adulthood. My parents, my grandmother, and my sister Debbie sat in the audience, with Debbie interpreting every word in ASL to my parents. During his speech, the valedictorian blended in an impromptu recognition of Debbie. He talked about the future and how at times it would be a struggle, but to keep focused and work hard. He must have assumed incorrectly that having a "handicap" would be a struggle and it would take extra effort to be successful. The audience in the auditorium erupted in applause as I beamed. On this day, my family—my parents in particular—had been singled out. At that moment I felt something new: pride.

MEANINGFUL CONVERSATIONS with my parents lacked substance, and for this I truly am sad. I often wonder: Did my move to Joseph City, when I was fourteen, play into this distance between us? Do parents and teens generally not communicate? Or was there another contributing factor—because my parents were deaf? Most of our conversations centered on sports: the failures and successes of the Los Angeles Dodgers, the Rams, the Angels, or my father's team, GGAAD.

Throughout the years my father shared some of the experiences he had had with the young deaf individuals or couples he counseled. I found it fascinating to be privy to their life difficulties, their family relationship dynamics. I could identify with how it was to grow up in a mix of sound and silence, void of any real conversations. More than 90 percent of deaf children are born into hearing families. The vast majority of those hearing families cannot communicate with their deaf children. Now, in my private practice at the hospital and group home, I see what an impact this lack of common language has on my students, rendering them unable to communicate their basic needs and often leading into numerous misunderstandings. Adolescents, deaf or hearing, are starving for communication at every level. This is a greater issue among deaf children who are born into hearing families as opposed to deaf children within deaf families. For this reason, it is with rare exception that deaf kids from deaf families seek out my practice.

DURING THE YEARS IN JOSEPH CITY living apart from my parents, somehow an eight-volt transistor radio fell into my hands. It became my habit to listen to it at night as I went to sleep. I would plug in an earpiece and tune in to a KOMA broadcast out of Oklahoma City.

Music had intrigued me as a youngster, but it had never occurred to me to ask my parents for a radio. It certainly would not have occurred to them. Being deaf, my parents never thought to have a radio or turntable in the house. The value of music had been lost on them—or so I had thought. When I was about eleven, I remember my surprise when my parents brought home an old Philco, a bulky brown radio larger than a typewriter. It had two dials: one for adjusting the volume and the other for selecting AM stations. I had at my fingertips the sounds of Dion and the Belmonts, Elvis Presley, Buddy Holly and the Crickets, and Roy Orbison. I was jazzed!

It was years later, as a teenager living hundreds of miles away from my parents, when I developed a real love for music, since the Oklahoma City station could be heard only at night. The British Invasion introduced Peter and Gordon, Gerry and the Pacemakers, Herman's Hermits, and, best of all, the Beatles. Every month a group played at the armory or legion hall in Holbrook. Those nights were filled with fun and frolic.

After I moved in with my grandmother, my contact with deaf people nearly vanished from my life. Even in the last year of living with Mom and Dad, I had started to detach from the Deaf community. By moving to Joseph City, my ties were severed. I was absorbed by the hearing world, feeling a newfound freedom. I met my first girlfriend. I made lifelong friends.

The deaf country in which I had lived so long faded away. It would be fifteen years before I returned.

9

Soul Searching

I DECIDED to go to Eastern Arizona College, a community college in Thatcher, home of the Gila Monsters. Thatcher is a small, predominantly Mormon community known for its cotton, about two hours east of Phoenix. My father's brother Ed lived in Thatcher with his family, so I would not have to live in the dorms. Suddenly, I had a new family. Sort of. The family consisted of Uncle Ed and Aunt Ellamae and my four cousins, two boys and two girls, who to me were just more children underfoot. I was a college student with a new social life, and that was my priority.

Uncle Ed was the dean of the vocational education department at Eastern Arizona College. Knowing I enjoyed sports and that I had some experience writing sports articles for my high school newspaper, he got me a job as the sports editor for the college newspaper—a perfect match for me. I worked the booth high above the football field every Friday night watching the play-by-play action. After the game I reported the game highlights and results to the sports departments of the United Press International and the Associated Press. My other responsibilities were to typeset the stories for printing. Each Thursday we took the prepared type to the local printer for Sunday's edition of the *Gila Monster.* Although I enjoyed my time as the sports editor, I still was in party mode and wanted to be with my friends. I was not quite mature nor responsible enough to continue working for the paper. In a short time, my partying ways caught up with me and my journalism instructor asked me to leave the paper.

Unbeknownst to me, my time at Eastern and living with my uncle would be short-lived. One evening when I arrived back at my uncle's home and walked into the living room, there was my father. My jaw dropped, and I was at a loss for words. As I looked at my uncle and over to my father, both unsmiling, I knew in my head what this was about. This was not a pleasure trip for my father.

Uncle Ed began by summarizing the list of antics that were reason for my removal from Thatcher. As Ed talked, I signed to my father, paraphrasing what Ed had said. This felt like I was loading the rifles for my execution. My father spoke. "I'm disappointed in you."

The following morning my father and I drove back to Fullerton.

In December 1969, at age nineteen, I was drafted into the Army. I arrived in Albuquerque, New Mexico, to report for duty. I was grouped with some older guys. While waiting to board a plane to Monterey, California, we headed to the nearest bar for a drink or five. I was the youngest while the others were in their early twenties. Because I was not yet old enough to drink, we plotted that I would arrive after the others had found a seat and ordered their drinks. As they were being served, I would join them. As expected, the server assumed I was twenty-one and took my order as well. Without hesitation, I asked for a screwdriver. By the time we boarded the plane, none of us was feeling any pain.

We arrived at Fort Ord, about a two-hour drive south of San Francisco, early on a Saturday morning. One of the drill sergeants escorted us to the barracks to sleep for the night—or more accurately, until five in the morning, when I was jolted out of a dead sleep by the sound of screaming. A man in a green uniform wearing a brown Smokey the Bear hat screamed at us, "ATTENTION!" I was just coherent enough to leap from my bed and stand at, what I would loosely call, attention. Scared and disoriented, in a flash, I heard my father yelling "David!" in his booming voice that meant "Come here!" I stood in front of this tall figure, who looked down at me with an angry face. I barely made eye contact with him. My father's voice went from booming to a lower octave as he spoke, querying me about the money I had taken from my mother's purse earlier in the day. But no, it wasn't my father; it was the drill sergeant.

Before I joined the Army, I hadn't been a political creature. Like many of my peers, I'd voiced my opposition to the war in Vietnam; I'd objected to harsh marijuana laws that put people in prison for five to ten years for possession; and I'd participated in a number of love-ins. I'd also come across the John Birch Society, which touted anti-communist teachings. I'd read the writings of Robert Welch, one of the society's founders: *The Blue Book of the John Birch Society* and *The Politician,* otherwise known as *The Black Book.* Not only was the society antigovernment, it also opposed aspects of the civil rights movement, claiming its leaders were communists. I wholeheartedly rejected their philosophy.

Armed with my liberal beliefs, I quickly learned I wasn't military material. Oftentimes I said I was on my way to sick call to see a doctor, but instead of reporting to the clinic, I changed into my civvies, jumped onto a bus, and went into Monterey. There was a small two-room office in the quiet part of town in an obscure building off the main street. The office provided counsel to those seeking alternatives to joining the Army. I sometimes showed up—not often, but once in a while—to discourage my peers from enlisting.

I also did not spend much time training for combat. Instead, it was easier to find me in Monterey, Carmel, or Salinas, or even San Francisco. Other times, I was simply AWOL. Adventures included Phoenix, where I was detained and returned to Fort Ord. Then there was San Diego where again, I was arrested and returned to Fort Ord. I got the great idea to return to Phoenix, and this time it took them two months to catch me. This last time I was cooked. I spent twenty-eight days in the stockade. Upon release, I was reassigned to a holding company to await discharge, which occurred at the end of September 1970. It would be labeled general discharge under honorable conditions. They stamped my papers: Unsuitable for Military Life.

Now I had to weigh my options. Should I return to Fullerton and live with my parents? Or should I return to Holbrook, Arizona? I decided to bypass Fullerton. Instead, I arranged to live with my buddies in Holbrook. I did not really discuss my discharge with my parents or my sisters, since I had very little contact with them. I was very happy to have been discharged and be with my friends once again. When I talked with anyone, I gave a generic reason as to why I was out of the service in less than two years: I simply said the war in Vietnam was winding down and that many soldiers were coming back and being discharged. Although my close buddies knew of my behaviors while I was in the service, the story was told more as my manipulating the system to my advantage. I went AWOL twice; I never made it out of basic training. I simply learned and understood what I needed to do to get a discharge. I never considered myself a failure, because I had beaten the system.

I thought I might see if I was suited for romance, maybe even something permanent. Upon returning to Holbrook, I found my high school buddy Jack seriously courting a girl who had a best friend named Cindy. Cindy's mother had known my mother since they were little girls growing up in Joseph City. I knew Cindy's brothers, Mike and Tim. Our friendship grew, and when Jack decided to get married in June 1972, Cindy and I followed suit soon after, a month later.

We decided to get married in the local Mormon Church in Holbrook, a decision that delighted my parents and my grandmother but not Cindy's father. "I will buy you an entire house of furniture if you elope," he said. He made it clear to us that we, especially Cindy at seventeen years old, were not ready to marry. The way I saw it, marrying in the Mormon Church was a convenience. But some of my family members saw it as a sign that the sheep had returned to the flock. Not quite. The Mormon Church was cheap and would hold a lot of people. To Cindy's father's chagrin, we did go through with the wedding, with a ceremony in the Mormon Church. We took the furniture anyway.

UP TO THIS POINT IN LIFE, I had experienced very few moments when someone saw something in me. It was hard for me to see that myself. My life had moved in fits and starts: finishing up my childhood without parents, starting college and dropping out, and signing up for the Army and then getting thrown out. I realize today that all changed in early spring 1972, when I worked as a receptionist at the Arizona Department of Transportation. That's when I met Barbara Pritt, executive secretary to the district engineer.

Barbara could pull out of me stories about my youth, like my mishaps as a babysitter; or my mischief (my juvenile delinquency, if you want to put a fine point on it); like my understanding of my interpreting duties; my adventures in Deaf culture, which were fascinating to Barbara. She was all ears when I told her about the time in the early 1960s when my dad and his friend drove out to Utah to pick up a bunch of out-of-date Western Union teletype machines they hoped to convert to teletypewriters for deaf people. Understandably, I was curious when I had seen how excited my father was. However, once we were home with the old Western Union machine, my curiosity quickly changed to abhorrence when he hooked up the machine in his office, which shared a common wall with the den where I slept. One morning, the teletypewriter cranked into action.

KA-CHUNK-KA-CHUNK-KA-CHUNK!

I flew off the couch.

My dad had no sympathy for me. He simply adopted a "get-used-to-it" expression.

"But the noise is horrendous," I said.

He slipped a smile across his face, shrugged his shoulders, and signed, *I'm deaf, and I can't hear it.*

Barbara loved it when I signed. She encouraged me to sign more, which I did every time we crossed in the hallway by making a casual salute meaning *hello,* or signing, *What's up?* One day she asked me to teach her the ASL manual alphabet. During lunch I taught her the alphabet, and she was a quick study. "If you do not know a sign for a word," I told her, "spelling out the word will suffice. People will understand you. Of course, spelling out every word . . . could be a boring conversation . . ."

I told Barbara about the time when I was a freshman at Sunny Hills High School and getting suspended for a couple days after pushing my teacher. I told her how I changed words and minimized some of the language the principal wanted to convey to my father. She looked at me with her head cocked to the side, and shook her head. I acknowledged it was not the best behavior, but it had worked for me.

Sometimes we laughed until tears poured from our eyes. Other times she'd absorb my tales with concern and newfound respect. She sensed that I must have become a very responsible person by an early age despite later antics. "You're Dennis the Menace," she said after one of my tales.

One day Barbara said, "David, you're not like the other people." It stunned me—I didn't think I had anything going for me. But she went on, "Think about leaving, going to the university, getting a degree in psychology." She detailed my skills and admired my ability to work with deaf people. "Your sign language is beautiful," she added.

I didn't say yes, but I did agree to think about it.

FOREVER SINCE I CAN REMEMBER, if I shopped or went to a ball game and I saw a deaf person, I made it a point to go over and chat awhile. One weekend afternoon while living in Holbrook, I was driving east on Hopi Boulevard toward "the hill," one of the landmarks of the town, when I noticed a car with California plates in front of me with two people signing. I was so thrilled to see another deaf person that I spontaneously waved my arms to attract their attention. It took them a few miles, but eventually the driver pulled over to the side of the road and into the parking lot in front of the Hilltop Café. I began to sign to the driver, who was looking into his rearview mirror. A broad smile lit up his face. He and his passenger jumped out of their car and joined me in the parking lot. We were like long-lost buddies. The driver introduced himself as Larry and presented his friend Ted. I introduced myself.

Where are you headed?

Missouri, they signed back. *To a bowling tournament.*

Larry asked if I was deaf. *No,* I said. *My parents are deaf.*

I explained that my parents lived in California and were Mel and Eileen Sorensen. Larry said he did not recognize their names, which did not surprise me. Yet through the years, I have run into many deaf people, especially older ones, who knew of my father.

We said our goodbyes and left grinning. I got into my car and sat for a while and thought about how comfortable it felt to sign to a deaf person again, and how much I missed interacting with deaf people.

Because of incidents like this, I did not totally disregard what Barbara had to say. I knew I had great people skills and that growing up with deaf parents and understanding the culture and language set me apart from many other people. Yet I did not truly understand the breadth of Barbara's words. After all, I had not come from educated stock. Although my father took some courses at the local community college and my mother attended Gallaudet College for several years, I simply could not imagine myself as a university student. I'd barely made it through high school. My brief stint at Eastern Arizona College had ended in disaster and embarrassment. It was apparent that academia and I did not mix.

The odds that I would act on Barbara's suggestion were fairly low. I had had no previous support or encouragement to attend. My grandmother had never spoken to me about college, and seldom was there a word uttered about furthering my education. I believe my grandmother did not think I was "college material," considering the trouble I had been involved throughout my teenage years. But I knew intuitively I was a smart person. I caught onto things quickly and could solve problems easily.

Barbara kept after me about college, and although I thought it was a nice idea, each time I made up excuses. College meant moving, and I was married to Cindy, who enjoyed living in Holbrook close to her friends and family. I assumed it was something she would not consider. Two months later, I was unexpectedly transferred from the receptionist desk to work in the field doing maintenance work.

By then my marriage was crumbling. Cindy had married me so she could move away from home. We fancied ourselves in love, but it was more like infatuation, short on deep connection and physical intimacy. We had set up house, and we spent most Sundays at Cindy's parents' house and played Rook with her brothers and sisters, who I loved. But soon in, we knew our marriage was in trouble. We had both been too young, and we were guilty of being ridiculously naive.

By the summer of 1975, Cindy and I agreed to part ways, which forced me to think about life changes. I knew I did not want to be a laborer all my life, and the seeds Barbara had planted made sense to me. I began to give some serious consideration to attending NAU. At age twenty-five, I enrolled as a freshman.

10
A Return

I STRUGGLED academically for the first three years at university. Some of the familiar problems returned. I did not know how to study, had poor time-management skills, and was not a particularly good reader. However, what hindered me the most was that I was still in party mode. If I could get out of doing my studies, I would.

I spent the first summer session settling in, making new friends, and partying with the old. I enjoyed the beautiful landscape surrounding Flagstaff. To the north, the San Francisco Peaks tower over the city. The mountain terrain empties into the high desert twenty miles to the east. To the west, the mountains gradually disappear over the next fifty miles into the low desert. To the south, the mountains drain into the beautiful red clay canyons of Oak Creek and Sedona. The region offered plenty of hiking trails and historic Native American sites like Walnut Canyon National Monument to the east of Flagstaff. I was more intent on exploring these treasures—school couldn't compete with the wanderer in me.

By the fall semester of 1975, I was a sophomore and still was not faring much better. As mentioned earlier, my little sister Christy had become pregnant. After my firm and loving plea to our parents on her behalf, she decided to keep her baby, and we all agreed that she would come to live with me for a while. I was installed in student family-living quarters, which consisted of a two-bedroom apartment with a small kitchen and living room. Christy moved in with the idea that this would be for only a few months. Having Christy there, plus a full load of classes, I continued to struggle to focus. I vowed to do my best to take care of her, and I think I did a good job.

One night she woke me up just before midnight. "David," she said quietly, "I think I need some licorice ice cream."

I roused myself from a deep sleep and got dressed. The two of us hopped in my car and headed to Baskin Robbins. We counted ourselves lucky it was open, and that they just happened to have licorice ice cream. We laughed about how crazy this was as we shared our bowls of ice cream together.

Back at the apartment, she heaved all over the kitchen floor. We just shook our heads. Christy apologized, and we cleaned up the mess. "That was a waste of good licorice ice cream," I said, and she laughed.

By fall 1976, we were both back in our parents' house in Fullerton. But my return to the country of the deaf was purely practical. Financial aid had run out, so I took a job at Knott's Berry Farm during the day, adding on extra four-hour shifts from 6 to 10 p.m. Monday through Friday. I then worked the graveyard shift at a nursing home for elderly developmentally disabled adults. Now I had focus: earn money, pay off my debts, and buy a truck and a motorcycle. Although I was back in the fold for the first time since I was fourteen, I saw very little of my sisters or my parents because I was working all the time. My privilege and my purpose were to live in their house without paying rent so I could get back on my feet financially and get back in school.

I think my parents were happy I was back, though our relationship had not changed. They had always said they wanted us to live with them, at any time. I believe they meant it. I also think they knew it would never happen. The whole idea was premised in Mormon philosophy, which stresses the value of family. On the other hand, my father's promise could have been an unconscious or conscious attempt to reconcile his separation from his family while attending school in another state. This time, though, I was an adult and they gave me no pressure about church. Christy had given birth to a baby girl named Jessica, and she split her time between living with our parents and Jessica's father's family. Even so, none of this registered enough to sway me from my goal: I wanted nothing more than to return to Flagstaff and resume school.

In the spring, I got word I had financial aid in place and could return in the fall. In the meantime, I worked, and worked some more, saving enough money to buy a used blue Chevrolet LUV pickup and a Kawasaki motorcycle. As part of my financial aid package, I had a work-study job at the Institute for Human Development. I tried valiantly to focus on my academics but still found myself off on weekend adventures. Despite my distractions, I was successful at school each step of the way. It was becoming easier. Having the independence growing up and into adulthood hadn't held me back; rather, it had shown me the way to be in charge of myself. In a strange and roundabout way, my father had been a good influence as someone who had been successful in school, formed his own athletic club, and served as president of the branch for deaf people at his church for many years. The man had initiative, and he could lead. Something had kicked in for me.

Something else was happening, too. It was becoming clearer to me that I was compelled to work with deaf people. The first time I remember feeling like I had to do this was during my first year at NAU, when I was chipping away at my bachelor's degree in psychology. I'd stumbled onto some education periodicals one afternoon and found myself reading an article about the Community Outreach Program for the Deaf in Tucson. The article outlined the services the agency provided and the demographics it targeted. I knew immediately that I wanted to be a part of this program. Because no telephone number was listed in the story, I called the operator. Once connected with the agency, I asked if any positions were available and, if so, if I could speak with the person responsible for hiring. The woman on the other end said they were looking for a person to work in a group home for developmentally disabled deaf adults. I immediately expressed interest and asked if I could apply for the job. Unfortunately, they felt that I did not have the experience needed with that population. I pleaded my case to the supervisor. I acknowledged that although I may not have had any direct experience, I had other qualifications. I rattled off that I had grown up with deaf parents and that I was a fluent signer. I'd completed some college coursework in psychology and sociology. At twenty-six years old I felt certain that I was mature enough to handle the job. To my surprise I was still not given the job because I didn't have enough "hands-on experience."

I THOUGHT IT WOULD BE A WHILE before I would try marriage again. I was willing to try love, but not marriage. In 1977, I met Donna on a personal development retreat by the Tonto Natural Bridge near Payson, Arizona, a small tourist community about eighty miles north of Phoenix. I was twenty-seven and still an undergraduate. The retreat was two miles off a state route. I turned off the main highway and onto a dirt road that wound down to a long, dusty path that came to a dead end in a small, densely covered valley. In the clearing stood a two-story Victorian built in the early twentieth century, now refurbished for retreats.

The Tonto Natural Bridge is a natural bridge that the constant flow of Pine Creek has carved out of limestone over many thousands of years. Climbing down to the river, I grabbed the hand railings installed along the steep canyon walls, preferring the more rugged route. Underneath the bridge was a massive cavern. I crossed the river numerous times, jumping over rocks and boulders. I balanced myself alongside the canyon wall to walk the river's side and explored tunnels and swung out over the water on a rope, feeling like Indiana Jones. The place had a beckoning quality, and I found myself climbing down into the canyon and traversing the river several times.

I met Donna at an evening icebreaker, which included a trust exercise in which were instructed to pair up and give massages. On that touchy-feely note, Donna and I decided to get to know each other better.

Within six months, I moved into her rented house in Holbrook. The following year we purchased a small home on a one-acre lot as an unmarried couple. At the time we thought it wasn't a big deal. We had both been married before and it was a pain and not worth the bother.

We'd flirted with the idea of having children, but it was a vague, open-ended dream. Within several months Donna became pregnant. Five months into her pregnancy, she miscarried, which devastated us both. However, within several months we discovered that Donna was expecting again, and our son, Jon Aaron Sorensen-Wagner, was born on Thursday, June 17, 1980.

WHILE I WAS GETTING MY DEGREE IN PSYCHOLOGY, I decided I wanted to be a counselor with deaf people. In order to be a counselor or do therapy, I needed to have a master's degree, and I wanted to get the degree at an out-of-state university because I wanted a change from Arizona. Oregon College of Education in Monmouth offered a graduate program in rehabilitation counseling for deaf people. By definition, rehabilitation counseling helps people who have emotional and/or physical disabilities to live independently. What appealed to me was that rehabilitation counselors work with clients to overcome the effects of disabilities on their ability to work or live independently. I wanted to specialize in doing that for those deaf people who needed such resources.

I had the skills, experience, and quite frankly a leg up, being a Coda. My gut told me not to work with adults but with children. I have often thought that my being a counselor was a reflection of my father, who was a lay counselor in his church and in the Deaf community. I preferred to be on the proactive side of the issues and work with children and adolescents as they transitioned into adulthood and developed successful lives.

As I finished my bachelor's and waited to be accepted into the master's program, Donna and I decided to move to Oregon, where

I got a job at the Oregon School for the Deaf in Salem. It was one of the very few schools in the United States that had rehabilitation counseling for deaf adults. This was the first deaf school at which I had ever worked, and I felt as if I had returned to my deaf roots. I walked around campus and talked with administrators and teachers who knew my father and went to Gallaudet with my mother. It became more of a reality when the children arrived at the school. When I saw how the children joined into activities and settled into their rooms, I realized this must have been what it was like for my parents.

My responsibilities were twofold: I was both teacher and aide in a primary classroom. For a couple of hours a day, I was assigned to work with two children, one of whom was deaf-blind, the other of whom was autistic. I also taught math and escorted the students to their various appointments on campus, such as physical therapy. I was not a stranger to working with individuals with autism or developmental disabilities, since I had worked with students who had these disabilities at NAU. However, I was new to working with deaf students in a residential school. I worked at the school through the spring, then through the summer I got into canning fruits and vegetables from our home garden.

After summer break I learned I had been accepted into the master's program at the Oregon College of Education; however, they did not offer any financial assistance. I met with various departments in hopes of getting assistance; I could not attend graduate school full-time without some help financially. My efforts were to no avail. I did not receive any grants, stipends, or scholarships. Disappointed, Donna and I decided to move back to Tucson, where I had been accepted into graduate school in a similar program at the University of Arizona. The counseling program had a great reputation, as did the sign language instruction and deaf studies program. I began my studies in the fall of 1982. The department awarded me a tuition waiver, free books, and a substantial monthly stipend for the next two and a half years. But Donna and I couldn't make ends meet with just a stipend, so I applied and was hired as a classroom aide in the elementary school at the Arizona State School for the Deaf and the Blind (ASDB).

In order to graduate, I was required to participate in a practicum and serve as an intern during my last two semesters. However, with no director or experienced professor to supervise my practicum and internship, I was assigned to a doctoral student with very little experience. We clashed over everything. If the problem wasn't my paperwork, it was my technique or the way I counseled deaf people. I decided not to argue with him and instead went directly to the division dean. I announced that I could not accept the doctoral student's limited knowledge of Deaf culture and would not accept him as my supervisor.

"Just because he's married to a deaf woman does not qualify him as a Deaf cultural or linguistic expert," I told the dean. "I grew up in a Deaf community. My parents are deaf. I have been a member of Deaf clubs. I have attended deaf churches. I have played on deaf softball teams. I am fluent in ASL. How much more knowledge of deaf people do I need?" I explained that I needed someone with more expertise than me, and only that person could appropriately assess my abilities.

My intention was not to come off as arrogant, although it could have been interpreted that way. I know now that many people, especially interpreters new to the field, have often referred to Codas as arrogant and know-it-alls.

The dean hired an outside consultant, Dr. Armin Turchek, who had been director of the rehabilitation counseling program but had retired the spring before I entered the program. Dr. T was well respected in the field. He was a former superintendent of a school for deaf students, had been published in various journals, and served on many national boards. He was also a Coda. Dr. T turned out to be a tall, thin, grandfatherly looking man. His soft voice was nurturing, like a warm blanket on a cold day. I was very much in awe of Dr. T, who was all business, very direct as to what his and my responsibilities were going to be for the semester.

Dr. T saw my potential. Each week he supervised my counseling and reviewed the videotapes with me. He provided his valuable knowledge and insight. As a young and inexperienced counselor, I had many things to learn. I wasn't the best student in the world, but he saw where I could go. He molded me into something better than I had been. In a short time, I graduated with a master's degree.

11

Transitions

After graduate school I continued working at ASDB. Work was going well, but I knew things were not well with me. I'd begun to withdraw from my family. If Donna was aware, she kept it to herself. I believe she was in denial, as was I. Regardless of the ever-growing chasm, we agreed to marry. We had been together for a long time, and Aaron was five years old. I do not remember whose idea it was to marry, but I guess it was by mutual agreement.

We married on Thanksgiving Day in 1985 at my grandmother's home in Mesa, Arizona, where she had moved. My entire family drove in a caravan from Fullerton for the event. My Uncle Jim, my mother's sister's husband, married us. Jim was a Mormon bishop in Mesa and had the authority to marry couples.

My grandmother lived in a small two-bedroom house with a living room large enough to host a small gathering. Thanksgiving Day was a warm and cloudless day, a typical autumn day in central Arizona. The affair was casual, and definitely not Mormon, and neither Donna nor I had the traditional bridesmaids or groomsmen. Everyone gathered in the living room, Jim in front to officiate with Donna and me standing before him. Jim held a book from which he read vows, and the ceremony lasted all of fifteen minutes.

The morning before the wedding was hustle and bustle preparing for a traditional turkey dinner with all the trimmings. Part of the Sorensen clan, Lori, Christy, and my brother-in-law John were enjoying beer outside because my grandmother did not allow "such refreshments" in her home. Everyone was talking, and it seemed everyone was enjoying each other's company, catching up on who was doing what. I had not seen my family for about six months, so it was nice to have the family gather again.

After the ceremony we helped set the tables with plates and silverware and food. We all took our places around the various tables before Jim blessed the food.

"Why did you get married after seven years?" someone asked.

"It was as good as any other day," I said.

We were all joking, but Jim said, "It is about time. The Lord will bless you."

Nearby in the next room, my parents sat signing to each other. Every so often, they would glance over to the activities around them, but then resume their conversation. Debbie had been the interpreter for the day—not continuously, but at times. All my sisters signed to let my parents know what was going on from time to time or fill them in when they had questions.

Donna never learned to sign. She understood that she needed to face my parents when she talked. She did, however, exaggerate her pronunciation, which always annoyed me. She seemed comfortable talking with my parents and most of the time their communications were fine. I would know when there were communication failures when my parents smiled and looked at each other. I would prompt her, telling her under my breath that they did not catch what she said. In stride, she would repeat herself. If there was a serious discussion, which rarely happened, I would interpret for Donna.

"The day turned out just like I thought it would be," I said to Debbie later. "I think everyone had a great time." What I didn't tell her was this, a truth I couldn't betray: Inside I was a mess.

The following spring, I began to consider that perhaps the emptiness I felt was not from my flawed relationship but rather from a lack of spiritual connectedness. Church was not the answer; I'd done my time in my formative years. I was searching for something else, something I couldn't name.

A friend suggested aromatherapy, which was just intriguing enough that I decided to travel to Bisbee to see an aromatherapist. Bisbee was an hour and fifteen minutes southeast of Tucson where Donna and I were living. On a late spring Saturday morning in 1986, when Aaron was six years old, I drove east on Interstate 10 into a sky of uninterrupted blue. I felt happy.

This drive took my mind back to our family vacations when I was little, when every year we packed up to visit our grandparents in Lovell and Joseph City. Usually, we would arrive at their home before dawn and park by the fence until my grandfather went out to the barn and milk his cows. Once we saw the lights come on in the house, we'd burst out of the truck into the house, and into our grandparents' arms. I had forgotten that part, the greeting. For too long, I had thought more about the leaving.

My route took me through Benson, a tiny town of a couple thousand with a train that ran through town. Next I came upon St. David, with a tree-lined main street, a Mormon Church, a monastery, and natural spring lakes. Next was Tombstone, "The Town Too Tough to Die," famous for its frontier copper mining, Wyatt Earp, and the gunfight at the OK Corral. As I continued on, the ride became smooth. A vast desert floor stretched out ahead of me, mountains to the east, endless flat desert to the west. Far off in the horizon I could make out the Huachuca Mountains. And then the road climbed higher into the juniper pines. The last five miles to Bisbee were on a two-way road that led to a tunnel built through the mountain. "Mule Springs Pass Tunnel," it said. As I went through I was amid steep canyon walls to the north and south, lesser canyons to the east and west. Now the hillsides were thick with juniper pines. Only a few homes were tucked into the slope of the north canyon and in the valley below, older wood homes probably built at the turn of the century. My first thought as I drove through the tunnel at Mule Pass was that I had left the twentieth century behind and had somehow escaped to the nineteenth.

In Old Bisbee, the streets were narrow, barely wide enough for two cars to pass. The buildings reminded me of the row houses in New York City and San Francisco. There were antiques stores, quaint cafés, record and bookstores, and crystal and bead shops. At the time, Bisbee had two beautiful old hotels, the Grand and the Copper Queen. The town had thrived in the early 1900s when the Phelps Dodge mining company owned much of the town's enterprise and employed most of the people. On this drive, instead, the town was emerging as a haven for artists.

I met the aromatherapist at a small café. She gestured for me to follow her outside, leading me across the street and up a flight of stairs of about 100 steps to her home, which was built into the side of a hill. Bisbee's veins and arteries are the steps that join the homes and streets. I told the aromatherapist of my need: I wanted to find something to fill the spiritual cavern within me.

Despite my awkward choice of words, she seemed to understand what I was trying to articulate. She placed colored rocks in my palm. Somehow these would determine the scents and aromas she would select for me. We touched on the issues of marriage, happiness, loneliness, and anger. After experimenting with various scents, she determined a particular scent that was not pungent; it was very subtle, pleasing to my senses, and light like lavender with a hint of mint. She asked me to be consistent in its usage and to be patient, and it would help me find peace. I was a bit incredulous regarding her approach, but I tried to listen and limit my questions. I left with a small bottle of the scent and her telephone number.

My car seemed to crawl home. The anticipation of my session had dissipated, and I felt a sort of dread. Filled with skepticism, I doubted aromatherapy was the key to unlock the happiness within me.

Loneliness set in in the days after that trip. Somehow Shirley MacLaine's autobiography *Out on a Limb* fell into my hands, and I became fascinated with her past-life regression. Perhaps this was the answer. I started seeking out individual names and resources from the back of her book. I called a psychic in Galisteo, New Mexico, and explained my quest. The woman referred me to a past-life regression expert, Alan, in Sedona, Arizona.

Before I committed to the trek north, I spoke with Debbie, who was also interested in nontraditional healing practices such as reflexology, homeopathy, and massage. "I'm struggling," I said, "I'm sad." I told her about the Shirley MacLaine book, which fascinated her. To my great joy, Debbie agreed to go with me and meet with Alan.

I called Alan, poured my heart out to him, told him of Debbie, and grilled him with questions about what would happen in the event that we met. We set up a time and date during the summer of 1986. The plan was to spend five days in a hotel in Sedona and meet with Alan daily. Alan would spend his mornings with me, and Debbie would take up his afternoons.

Sedona is only about a twenty-minute drive south of Flagstaff, which is situated in the largest ponderosa pine forest in the continental United States. As I made my descent off the plateau, the pine trees thinned out and made room for the majestic sycamore and cottonwood trees. I grew nostalgic, remembering lazy summer afternoons driving alone or with friends to Oak Creek's Grasshopper Point. We'd park, strap on backpacks, and trek up the river to a secluded spot where boulders, rocks, and trees protected us from the public. The beautiful blue skies and the summer sun were perfect for nude sunbathing and swimming in the cool waters.

Alan's home was just south of the road by about a quarter-mile. Debbie and I parked in front of his pueblo-style home. The inside was spacious and light, decorated in a Southwestern motif with native rugs, R. C. Gorman and Tonita Peña paintings, and pottery.

Alan, a man of medium height, slightly robust and balding, greeted us with a handshake and a hug. His soft and comforting voice immediately put us at ease. We made small talk for a while and he offered us refreshments. We discussed what we could expect during the week and set up our appointment times. After several hours, we left to check into our modest hotel room in Oak Creek, a fifteen-minute drive away. As we drove Debbie and I processed our impressions of Alan and his home as well as our excitement at having begun our journey to reconciling body, mind, and spirit.

Early on the following morning, we woke to a cloudless sky. Debbie and I ate a light breakfast at a small café. Afterward, I dropped her off at the hotel and headed off to Alan's. As we talked, we meandered through his home until we came to a white room full of windows. The room temperature was warm, but comfortable. The only furniture visible was a long bed-like bench similar to a chiropractor's bench, a chair, and a small table. A white gown was draped on the bench.

"Please undress," Alan said, "and put on this gown."

He left the room. I did not know why I needed to put on the gown, but I refrained from asking any questions. I dutifully put on the gown and sat waiting for Alan to return. When he arrived, he asked me to lie down on the bench.

"Are you comfortable?" he said as he arranged a pillow under my head. He placed himself on the chair directly behind my head and began to explain he would slowly induce me into a trance-like state. As the trance intensified he would ask me questions and I was to respond using free association, saying whatever came into my head first. I was to be as vivid as I could in describing people, environments, color, time of year, feelings, and senses.

In the 1970s, I had experimented with transcendental meditation. It was a technique used to bring a person into a deep contemplative state, thereby issuing forth a feeling of spiritual happiness or a state of tranquility. I felt a similar response after my session with Alan. Although the entire experience seemed to have lasted only minutes, when I looked at my watch, I realized hours had passed.

"I think you would benefit more fully from therapy," Alan said. "You are holding back. You need to relax into the experience and not censor your descriptions." He handed me the transcript of our session. "Rewrite this in your own words," he said. "That way you can better connect to what happened."

I left Alan's home feeling relaxed and, for a lack of a better word, enlightened. As I stepped outside, everything seemed more vivid.

The warmth of the day enhanced my mood. The flowers' colors radiated. The day's sounds were magnified. As I drove back to Oak Creek grinning, I was aware of people on foot and in automobiles passing me. When I arrived at the hotel, I crossed paths with Debbie. Enigmatically, I smiled but did not elaborate on my experience. She sensed my mood, and we agreed to speak over dinner about our day with Alan.

I met with Alan three more times that week. Each day he began by drawing me into a state of the subconscious. As I slipped deeper into that faraway place, my past lives became more vivid and alive. I've been fairly reticent about revealing my past-life encounters with others because I consider them highly personal. I have shared these stories only with intimate friends. One of the most powerful experiences I had during the week occurred when I surrendered so deeply to a subconscious state that I began to feel ill. I saw nothing but dim light. I felt like I was getting a migraine; my head throbbed. I asked Alan to close the session. He insisted that I continue. I grabbed my head and writhed in pain. Again, I begged Alan to cease this session. Again he refused.

As I fell further away from consciousness, images began to formulate. I began to see several people. I saw myself talking with a man; I was holding a gun. From our clothing I hazarded a guess that it was the early 1800s. It was a cloudy, early morning. I could see that around me were green grass and sycamore trees, the ground was thick with green bushes. The temperature was nondescript, neither hot nor cold. I could see two figures not far from where we stood. A woman was deep in conversation with another man, who also held a gun. I watched helplessly as I began to approach the other man. He, too, advanced toward me. I watched us speak briefly but could not make out the words. We then turned around with our backs to each other.

Beyond us stood a woman. Her hair was black and tucked neatly into her hat. I saw she was crying, and in her hand was a handkerchief. She watched us without interfering. We were now pacing off in opposite directions. My opponent turned and before I could even raise my gun, he fired. Something in my head exploded. I fell, in slow motion, to the earth. The woman stood alone crying. The shooter looked on. The man with whom I had been conversing came running to my aid. I lay on the ground, and the pounding in my head suddenly vanished.

When my week with Alan ended, I felt at odds with myself. On the one hand, I'd had a dramatic week exploring the inner reaches of my mind, but on the other, I now had to reconcile my past with my present. What I had wanted was an answer. I had wanted someone to tell me what I should do about my marriage.

BY THE SUMMER OF 1987, my divorce from Donna was finalized and I was resettling in my work at ASDB and personal life. I had worked at ASDB for five years, and I felt it was time for a challenge. Things were settling down in both my personal life and career. At one point after obtaining my graduate degree, I told myself I was done with school, no more. But these transitions made me realize that I wanted to go back to school; I was not finished. I decided to apply to NAU's doctoral program in educational administration and leadership, with the aim of combining my counseling background with administrative skills so I could hold a state-level or school-level position. My plan was to attend the university during the summers and continue working at ASDB.

I was accepted into the program at NAU in 1990. By now, I was more adept at navigating academia. I expected that the doctoral program would be rigorous, so I took it easy the first and second summer sessions by taking only one class per session. I attended full-time sessions in Flagstaff for five summers in a row.

I enjoyed the doctoral program immensely. Mike Miles, my committee chair, helped me gather a team to supervise my studies. One member of the team was a master of statistics, a skill I came to really appreciate as she helped me edit my dissertation on Deaf culture and school discipline. Two other professors on my committee helped me bounce around ideas. We were a great team. If any problem surfaced, Mike would take care of it. He was more than my committee chair—he was like a grandfather, father, and cheerleader all rolled into one. He'd taught at NAU for decades and knew the ins and outs of the program. He also was a kind soul who spoke to me in soft tones. From this point, my career took a turn. I enjoyed my studies, and there was no looking back.

During these years, I visited my parents several times a year, and when I did, I would tell them all about my doctorate studies. I was proud of what I was doing and enjoyed telling them about my classes and how the knowledge would coincide with my plans in administration. I told them I hoped to do my part in advocating for deaf people, educating hearing individuals and agencies. When I talked, they smiled but did not ask questions. The concept of what I was doing and of higher education seemed foreign to them. I believe my mother did have some idea because she attended college for several years, but mostly I was left unsure, not knowing how they processed this.

By this time I was working as the Nevada State Coordinator for the Deaf in December 1996. It was all pretty overwhelming for them. I know they were proud of me and my accomplishments and my decision to work with deaf people, but they never said, *We are proud of you.* I knew they were, but I wanted them to say it to me. I was the only person in the family to pursue a career in the Deaf community.

During my second year at NAU, I encountered Susie, a gentle-hearted deaf woman with a wonderful sense of humor. I had first met her when she worked in the dorms at ASDB. In between, she had gone back to school and completed her master's degree in education. Susie had gone through some pretty horrific times. She was born with a mild form of cerebral palsy, and she was placed in an institution for people with learning disabilities. As it turned out, she wasn't developmentally disabled; she was only deaf. As soon as this was ascertained, Susie's life changed dramatically. She was still a child; however, the early years of isolation had done damage to Susie's psyche. She applied to NAU and was accepted during my second year of study. Although I had a head start, Susie was determined to graduate with me.

That did indeed happen in December 1996, when the commencement ceremonies were held in the NAU Skydome on a cold but cloudless afternoon. The Skydome was packed, with only a handful of families like my own. I almost felt like I was back in high school. Families were cheering their children, and it was fun. Susie and I sat in the front row right in front of the speakers and presenters. Unlike when I graduated from high school, I was now graduating from a program that put interpreters on the platform. The scene was so different from the day when my sister sat next to my parents in the bleachers interpreting just for them. From the front row, it was hard to pick out where my family was sitting in the crowd, but every so often, I would glance up at them, and they would be smiling. How I had come almost full circle, from just squeaking by to earning a doctorate with honors.

PART FOUR
Finding Home

12

I'm Professionally Deaf

A CHUBBY kid sat at a desk in the hallway, just outside the Community Hour room at the end of the hallway. He had been separated from the other students because of lack of cooperation and a vicious attitude. On this day in 1984, I was the new hire at ASDB, and there was more that I didn't know than I did. Which is to say, I was a magnet for pranks as the kids tested their boundaries with me.

I walked down the hall and came to a stop at his desk. I did not sign to him. I stared at him with a smile; I knew why he was there. He began to sign, assuming I was a hearing person who could not understand his language.

School is shit, he signed with a smile. *That teacher is a bitch.* I said nothing.

You're a jerk, he signed.

I was careful not to react, although inside I was completely amused. I waited until he'd had his fun, and signed, *Are you finished?*

The look on his face was priceless. His jaw dropped when I continued, *I can sign fluently. My mother and father are deaf.* I smiled wryly. *I think you need to accompany me to the principal's office.*

He did not argue.

"I WANT TO COMMUNICATE WITH MY MOTHER," said the older woman standing before me in the classroom at Northland Pioneer College in Holbrook. The woman worked as a nurse at the community hospital in Holbrook, and her deaf mother, Vy, a petite woman in her mid-seventies, lived with her and her family. As a young girl, Vy had attended the South Dakota School for the Deaf. The daughter had only rudimentary skills in sign language, but she wanted to learn more. She had come to a class at Northland Pioneer College, where I was working as the first-ever ASL instructor.

That job, which I started in the fall of 1977, was my first real taste of working in the Deaf community. The weekly evening classes were small, with only ten students, give or take, who ranged in age and ability. Some of my students were totally new to ASL, while others knew how to fingerspell.

Sometimes Vy accompanied her daughter to class, and all the students found the chance to try out their skills with a deaf person to be a real treat while also learning firsthand about Deaf culture. Vy was appreciative because she was somewhat isolated in her life. No one in her family knew how to sign other than her daughter with her rudimentary skills. I was struck with compassion for how much it touched her to be brought out of her isolation. The two of us shared our experiences growing up, she as a deaf person, me as Coda, and we found many similarities. After the first semester, Vy stopped attending class for health reasons. I visited her at her home in Holbrook to see how she was doing and to offer assistance in any way. I never did hear or see from her after the visit.

AT THE SENIOR CENTER IN HOLBROOK, I taught sign classes using the old standard text, *A Basic Course in American Sign Language,* which is considered a classic and is no longer used in many sign classes, as there are newer books and digital media for teaching sign language. I taught mostly conversational sign language and did not teach grammar or syntax, as they do today. Today's ASL classes are much more structured and are taught as a foreign language. My approach was to teach words and phrases through games and field trips. We went to cafés, grocery stores, and the local park. The games we played included word games in which each student came up with a sign and the next student had to add a sign plus the previous sign. Sometimes students had to memorize five, six, and even seven signs, and it was fun. Seniors would laugh and tease each other when they could not remember a word or a sign.

BECAUSE MY SISTER DEBBIE WAS FLUENT IN ASL and Deaf culture, she had two foundational skills important to becoming an effective interpreter. To bolster her already strong communication skills, she attended California State University at Northridge. At this time I was married to Cindy and working and living in Holbrook. Debbie took some interpreting and sign language courses. Laden with this knowledge, she accepted an interpreting position at Golden West College, a small college near her home. Debbie said she enjoyed being an interpreter but felt she could not make a living at it. This was in the early 1970s when ASL interpreters were not paid well. There were certainly no retirement or health benefits. When she was not interpreting a class, she was not paid.

Interpreters at the time were not yet considered professionals, but were regarded as classroom aides or helpers. The status of interpreters has evolved dramatically throughout the past few decades. There are professional interpreter associations such as the Registry of Interpreters for the Deaf (RID) and national organizations like the National Association for the Deaf (NAD). RID is a national organization that represents professional deaf and hearing interpreters. NAD, on the other hand, is a powerful civil rights organization that works to ensure equal rights for deaf and hard of hearing people. It is also more of a grassroots organization run by deaf people.

In less than two years, Debbie became disenchanted with working as an interpreter and decided to make a career change. The change in jobs foretold the end to Debbie's interpreting and work within the Deaf community. Debbie enjoyed working as an interpreter; however, like many other Codas, interpreting was her first and last job in service to the Deaf community. My family is typical in this regard, as most Codas do not go work in the Deaf community, even now. I have talked to many Coda friends throughout the years, and most shrug and say they were burned-out or felt they had done their share of interpreting and did not miss working with deaf people.

MY FIRST OPPORTUNITY TO WORK directly in counseling a deaf person was with an autistic sixteen-year-old deaf Navajo boy. I was working on my bachelor's degree at NAU when a job opened up working with developmentally disabled youth at the Institute for Human Development in Flagstaff. This young man had significant behavioral problems such as masturbating in public and stimming by pressing his fingers into his eyes; he also struggled with his communication skills. We worked hard as a team with this young man. My role was to teach sign language to him and his fellow students, as well as modify his behaviors. We stopped the "public thing," helped him reduce his stimming, and drastically increased his communication skills. The work we did together was challenging and rewarding, and it provided me a solid first step toward my professional career.

This experience gave me a thirst for more. I was starting to see I could make a difference, so at the end of my sophomore year at NAU, when a coworker suggested I work at the Chinle Valley School for Exceptional Children in Chinle, Arizona, on a Navajo reservation, I grabbed it. This was my first role as a program administrator.

I took a day off from my studies, borrowed a friend's green 1973 Chevy Impala, and drove the two and half hours to Chinle. It was already warm that Friday morning in mid-May. I chose the scenic route heading north. After about an hour, I turned onto a reservation road that led me past the historical homes of the Hopi people in Old Oraibi, Second Mesa, and First Mesa. I drove through Keams Canyon on my way to Chinle.

When I arrived, my coworker Marie introduced me to the director, Clara, a short, rather full-sized, older woman who spoke with a Spanish accent. Clara was warm but firm. She and I hit it off well, and I was quickly hired as summer program manager to coordinate academic programs for ten adolescent hearing Navajo boys and girls with various developmental disabilities.

When the summer break began, I packed my gear and moved to Chinle, where I shared a three-bedroom, sixty-eight-foot yellow trailer with Marie and a photographer named Tom, who taught high school in Los Angeles. At that time, I had long blond hair and a bushy beard, and my favorite attire was sandals and shorts, drawing much teasing from the Navajo women. I was one of only four nonnatives working at the school. My responsibilities as program manager included developing daily and weekly educational plans that coincided with cultural values. These included developing a vegetable garden and how to care for animals. We had a cow, horse, and goats to feed and take care of. There were daily trips to the canyon, a short drive away, to have lunch. I was also responsible for hiring local people as aides. One was Norma, a young Navajo teenager. The school also had a program to hire "grandmothers" to work with the students. One grandmother and Norma, both native Navajo speakers, had the responsibility to implement the daily and weekly schedule.

That summer, we made sand paintings and jewelry with the children. The program also included physical education and animal husbandry, my favorite. We planted a garden of corn, beans, and tomatoes. Oftentimes we would picnic at Canyon de Chelly.

I believe my exposure to different cultures (and having deaf parents) allowed me to grasp some of their difficulties traversing two cultures. Many Navajo children were being sent to boarding schools off the reservation, where they were punished for using their Navajo language. In many ways, deaf people and Native Americans have journeyed a similar path.

While there, I was honored when asked if I would participate in a coming of age ceremony for one of my students, a young teenage girl's passage from childhood to womanhood. Toward the summer's end I was also invited to participate in a healing ceremony for a coworker's ill father, who lived over an hour by vehicle north of Chinle, accessible only via washboard roads. I was received with warm hospitality, but when I was asked to participate in the ceremony, I hesitated. I hadn't understood I would be part of it, especially as a white man.

Seeing that I had many questions, the medicine man who was preparing the ceremony walked me to a tepee, where he described in great detail what to do: how to enter the tepee, where to walk once I entered, where each person was to sit, and how long the ceremony would last. Still, I felt uneasy because I was expected to participate in something so unfamiliar to me. I decided to leave before the ceremony began, and I confided this to my coworker, who agreed to drive me back to Chinle. Very likely I offended the family by leaving. It was years later, after much more life experience, that I understood the privilege I had passed up.

When the time came to return to my studies, I did not want to leave. The time I'd spent in Chinle learning the ways of the Diné (or "people") had been a humbling experience. I had stayed on the Navajo reservation longer than I expected. How many people would have the opportunity to learn or participate in ceremonies, feel a connection to the earth, understand another culture's idea of disability, and learn rudimentary skills (at best) in a new language? I was immersed into another culture, and I appreciated the connection I made with the people I met.

MY MOTHER'S ALMA MATER was the Arizona School for the Deaf and the Blind in Tucson. So when I started working there the year before I graduated from the University of Arizona, I felt as if I had come full circle. I had developed professional skills, gained experience in personal relations, honed my counseling practices, and made new lifelong friends. But I had not been part of the Deaf community for more than fifteen years—not since I'd left home at age fourteen. Despite my work in Oregon, it wasn't until I started working at ASDB, though, that I felt I had rejoined a community from which I had been estranged.

At ASDB, I was welcomed by teachers who had once taught my mother. Many of her friends were still employed at ASDB. One was

Bev and her husband, Frank, who embraced me wholeheartedly when they found out who I was. *Your father was a good basketball player,* Frank signed. Bev added, *Your mother was a sweetheart.*

Then there was John in the vocational department who had once been my mother's boyfriend. John did not go into detail other than signing, *Your mother was a pretty girl.* John did share that he once visited my mother and met her parents in Joseph City during Christmas break from school. John did not divulge any information other than, *Eileen's parents were strong Mormons* (he emphasized *strong*). My guess was John did not want to say anything that would go back to my mother.

At ASDB, I had instant friends. I was a Coda, I could sign and I understood the culture. Even today, although it has been more than eighteen years since I worked there, I still feel a kinship with the school and faculty that remain. It was at ASDB that I felt received into the Deaf community once again.

I REALIZED MY PASSION HAD ALWAYS BEEN with counseling, especially with young people. As I said, I may have inherited the counseling gene from my father, who often counseled his church congregants. When it came to counseling young Mormons, my father was available any day or night of the week. Once a young man in his mid-twenties knocked on our door on a Saturday morning. As I opened the door I recognized him. He signed, *Hi, David, how are you?* He asked if my father was in, and I walked him into my father's office. He smiled and my father closed the door for privacy. My father later told me the young man was struggling with his marriage and employment, but did not go into detail.

Another time, when I was about thirteen, I was getting ready for bed when a young couple knocked on the door at nine o'clock in the evening. I opened the door, and they asked to see my father. I walked them into the living room where my father was sitting. I had never met this couple and my father never divulged the details of these conversations, but he sometimes would tell me about the scope. *They come to me for relationship advice,* he would say. *Or sometimes to help them with their children. Some are angry with their parents because the parents don't learn how to communicate with them. Sometimes it's money. Or work.*

So in the fall of 1984, when I got promoted to full-time counselor at ASDB, I was thrilled. I'd been hired as an educational assistant just one year before, until I completed my counseling internship and graduated in December 1984. My role was to work with middle school and high school students, and my main task was to provide counseling to students who might have behavioral issues. I was also involved in taking a lead role in developing and sponsoring extracurricular activities such as student government, Native American Club, and a boys group.

I enjoyed working with students one-on-one, but I have learned throughout the years that working in a holistic environment proves more rewarding and satisfying. In that scenario, the deaf person has all-deaf teachers, coaches, and counselors, creating an environment around him or her that promotes more integrated learning. For one semester I had a dozen boys in a group. The main purpose was to look at the societal and cultural differences and similarities between boys (men) and girls (women). We performed projects such as cutting out men's ads and women's ads in magazines and discussing what they portrayed. Once we completed that project, we did a presentation for the middle school. In the Native American Club, which represented a large section of our students, we blended culture into our activities, such as making fry bread for lunch. The club participated in many community events, including the Mariachi Festival or Tucson Meet Yourself, big-draw events in Tucson. Then there was the ASDB Powwow, in which the entire school participated with arts and crafts. The ASDB library also hosted readings of Native American literature and provided interpreters. The event drew parents from all over the state who brought art and crafts for sale. Each year, nearly 1,000 people gathered for powwow dances and songs.

ARMED WITH A DOCTORATE after six years of study and thirteen years at ASDB, I was ready to make my break. It was 1996 and time for the next challenge. I learned that Prescott College was hiring for a position with its special student services. The main role was to keep the college in compliance with the Americans with Disabilities Act, which had been enacted in 1990, and to coordinate services for students with disabilities. At the time, Prescott was home to about 30,000 people. The town is known for its annual rodeo, which attracts thousands of people every Fourth of July.

This was my first interview in over thirteen years, and I was rusty. I did not get the job. Afraid of a repeat performance, I decided to go to the University of Arizona's career education program to learn how to interview. I went faithfully twice a week for about six weeks. During the program, I applied for a position as the state coordinator for deaf people in Carson City, Nevada. I was selected as one of two finalists for the position.

The first finalist, who happened to be a friend of my father's, suddenly withdrew and accepted another job. Simultaneously, I was asked to re-interview at Prescott College. Now that I had taken a job-interviewing class, I was no longer lacking in confidence. When I was offered the Carson City position, I was thrilled to think that I might actually have the choice between two positions. To my delight, I indeed was offered the job at Prescott. The director of personnel at Prescott told me that I'd had a strong interview and my responses to the committee's questions were clear and to the point, and that I'd demonstrated an easy confidence. "You were a different person during this interview," the director said.

The preparation at the career center had paid off. Ultimately, the pay that Prescott College offered was not to my satisfaction. I asked if I could teach a class or two and have free time during my schedule. Prescott agreed to my terms, but the salary was still not enough. The Nevada position appealed to me because it offered the potential to make changes within the system, educate hearing professionals, and develop and expand services for deaf people in education, vocational training, and advocacy. I would be state coordinator for the state rehabilitation agency, which included working with other agencies to set up programs and services to support deaf people and to develop policies and procedures for teaching sign language in schools and universities. I was also to assist in developing a training program for interpreters, and be groomed to take over the telecommunications programs. Plus, the salary was significantly higher. I accepted the job, bid farewell to my family at ASDB.

After I settled into my position in Nevada, I was told that under no circumstances should I seek funding from the Nevada legislature for our deaf services. My supervisor was unbending on this. She made a point to lay down the rules before I completed my first week. Very quickly, it became clear that her priority was assisted living and not deaf services. My hands were tied, so I launched myself into writing grant proposals.

I had been successful in receiving several grants that paid for a lift van for a senior citizen center in Winslow, Arizona, a start-up fund for both a charter school in Tucson and the day-care center at ASDB, and funding to produce the documentary *Handicapped Women in Non-Traditional Work Roles.* Yet grants were hard to come by. Over the years, the federal government had continued to made significant cutbacks in funding small programs. For example, I submitted a grant proposal while at ASDB for substance-abuse training and education. When my grant was reviewed, I was told it was written well but that another agency had received the funding. I was informed that the population who would benefit from the grant was too small and that the money would be better spent on a larger group of students. Grant awards are often given to disability groups in general, leaving advocates for deaf services to scramble for their piece of the pie.

I also took on a part-time position at Western Nevada Community College teaching ASL and deaf history. I have always enjoyed teaching, and when the dean of the language department at the college asked me to teach these courses, I jumped at the opportunity.

By February of 1996, it was clear that while I was Nevada's first state coordinator for deaf people, my boss thought of me only as a figurehead. I had proven myself to be hands-on on several successful projects, but most importantly, to be proactive for change, and the direction of my efforts was not what she really wanted. I was part of a committee that changed state education laws to include ASL in high school curricula. I was a member of an ad hoc group of interpreters that provided consistent, much-needed training to interpreters. I enjoyed working with different agencies throughout the state and learning about the political process, which got me acquainted with writing legislation and lobbying for bills. So I decided to draft an interpreter bill that would require all interpreters, no matter the setting, to meet certain qualification standards.

After investigating other state licensure laws, I crafted a bill similar to one passed in Utah. I met with the board of the Nevada Association of the Deaf in Las Vegas to present my work and field their questions. I left with a general consensus among the board that this licensure law was needed. One of the final details that needed to be ironed out was which organization, either the RID or the NAD, would control and manage the testing for interpreters.

I believed that designating the authority of testing, licensing, and monitoring to one organization could create friction, so I purposely did not name any particular organization in the bill. I hoped that the two organizations could each take on a different role in enabling the success of the bill, but I was wrong in thinking that any easy compromise would be met. Personally, I was in favor of the NAD's Nevada chapter assuming the responsibilities of testing and licensing.

Just before I found a legislator to sponsor the bill, my boss caught wind of the controversy about which organization would be in control. Believing that I had not involved enough deaf people in the process, she informed me that I had more work to do on the bill. I explained that, on the contrary, I'd worked with deaf people in Reno and had acquired the support of the Nevada Association for the Deaf, but to no avail. Unfortunately, the bill was shelved, and it would be years before it was readdressed. Frustrated, I reevaluated my situation in Nevada. My boss was distracted by developing an assisted living program, and so I didn't have the support I needed. This had neutralized my ability to accomplish something that would benefit the deaf people of Nevada.

But then I got wind of a project in the works, in which several deaf individuals were trying to build a small-scale program in Reno and Las Vegas that would advocate for deaf people in the state. We calculated that in order to get the two positions up and running, it would cost $300,000. This was a pittance compared with other monetary requests.

I decided to approach a man I knew as a leader in the Deaf community and who had strong ties to the Nevada Speaker of the House. If this grassroots organizer approached the speaker, he could get what was needed to start up the deaf services in Reno and Las Vegas. Because I knew that I had overstepped my bounds with my boss by initiating contact with a deaf grassroots organization and violating my agreement not to get involved in approaching legislators for funding, I had to inform this leader that I could not support him publicly. Nevertheless, he pulled through for me, securing the speaker's support for $300,000, which was awarded during the fall 1997 legislative session. This upset my boss, who suspected I had been involved somehow, but I danced around her questions. I then focused my attention on new legislation for a charter school bill. With talk of opening up science and vocational charter schools, I thought this would be a great opportunity for deaf professionals to organize and set up their own charter schools for deaf children. At the time, Nevada was only one of several states in the United States that still did not have a deaf school; until then, all education for deaf students was provided through local school districts.

My boss made it clear that I needed to remain neutral and not get involved. Nevertheless, during my lunch break or while away from the office, I met with deaf leaders, interpreters, parents of deaf children, and professionals who supported the concept of charter schools for deaf students. I met with legislators who were known supporters of charter schools to discuss my experience with legislation in Arizona. With the help of many others, we were able to gather a large contingent of interested deaf people and parents of deaf children for these important meetings. The support for charter schools was tremendous, and deaf people turned out in large numbers in both Carson City and at the governmental complex in Las Vegas. The legislators, who had supported a need for science and vocational charter schools, now added that there was a need for a school for deaf children. This was a significant coup. In the next legislative session, the charter school bill was passed, and a charter school for the deaf was established in Las Vegas in 1998.

This success also displeased my boss. I could see that my work as state coordinator was winding down. I had been in the position for shorter than a year, but I was antsy and eager to leave. While I was reading the want ads in the *Albuquerque Journal*, I discovered that the National Mental Health Institute on Deafness (NMHID) was hiring a program director at Desert Hills in New Mexico. I quickly called for the details and applied. After being interviewed by a panel of individuals from NMHID and the CEO of the center at Desert Hills, I was offered the job.

In my remaining six weeks as statewide coordinator, I found ways to get out of the office and visit programs in Reno and used all the personal leave I had available. In the final meeting with my boss, she said, "You are a strong grassroots supporter of the deaf, and that is admirable. I wish you luck."

I made a beeline for New Mexico.

13
On Being a Father, On Being a Husband

My one-year-old son lay in bed, lifeless, hooked to IVs and heart monitors, pale and small on the bed at Tucson Medical Center. I trembled when I reached out to touch his listless body. His skin burned with fever. I was on the verge of tears, ragged after driving from Salt Lake City to Flagstaff, then on to Tucson. The year was 1981, and we were moving from Oregon to Tucson. Donna and Aaron had traveled to Tucson a couple days ahead of me to settle in, while I had packed up the rest of our things in Oregon. I stopped in Flagstaff to check in by phone with Donna.

"Critical condition," Donna had said on the phone. "Spinal meningitis."

Those words reverberated through my mind through the endless stretch of highway from Flagstaff to Tucson. I had hopped right back into my U-Haul with my car in tow and driven four-plus frantic hours to the southern end of the state. My mother had contracted spinal meningitis when she was a child. The high fever was how she had become deaf. Was this going to be my son's fate as well? Would his world go silent? Even though I knew being deaf wasn't a bad thing, it broke my heart to see my son going through such pain.

At last, there in the hospital, looking at him, tiny and helpless, I considered how this could even happen. I tried as best as I could to dwell on the positive. My mother had been lucky. Many babies did not even survive spinal meningitis in the 1930s. As we watched and waited to see if Aaron would come through, I took a few moments to let my family know what was going on. I did not have a TTY to call my parents, so I called the house in Fullerton and talked with Christy. I agreed to keep her updated on his condition. Christy was twenty at the time and had a daughter of her own. I could sense her sadness over the phone.

"Is there anything I can do?" she asked.

"No, just please tell Mom and Dad," I said.

Then I called my other sister Debbie in Salt Lake. Debbie quietly absorbed this. We never broached the possibility of death.

I HAD NEVER PLANNED ON BECOMING A FATHER. Growing up, my abiding thought was freedom, not family. After all, I had been the not-so-attentive babysitter to four younger sisters. I had grown up with a father who seemed more interested in his role in the Mormon Church and the Deaf community.

It wasn't until Donna announced she was pregnant that the idea came into my head, but truthfully, it had rolled in right alongside a big ball of apprehension. Were we ready? Nonetheless, four months in, we had thrown ourselves into it, buying tiny baby clothes and decorating a nursery. This was when we were living in Holbrook.

One late evening, Donna's water broke. She had been cramping. We sped down the highway for the ninety miles to Flagstaff. Donna was rushed into the emergency room, where she gave birth to a baby girl about five months premature.

The baby could barely breathe. The doctor on call pulled me aside. "Your baby will not live," he said. He explained the various complications. In retrospect, I believe the doctor had sized us up, from our relationship to our financial situation to the costs we would incur trying to keep the baby alive.

"I recommend that the birth be recategorized as a miscarriage," he said with a mix of sympathy and practicality.

Intellectually I could see that the doctor was right, and I agreed. In her hospital room, I filled Donna in on the doctor's recommendation. "I understand what needs to happen," she sobbed.

I sat down on the bed next to her and stroked her arm to console her. "I want to name her Annie," she said.

Within a short time, Donna became pregnant again. This time with a surgical procedure and bedrest, she carried the baby for seven months. On June 17, 1980, we welcomed Jon Aaron heartily into the world. I was in the birthing room for the entire labor.

Aaron was an extremely good baby despite the times he became sick and colicky. Once when he was particularly finicky, we jumped into the car and drove all the way to Show Low, Arizona, a small, forested community in the White Mountains about thirty minutes south of Holbrook. We had heard that the motion of driving could settle a baby. It was true: When we arrived home, Aaron was sound asleep.

JUST SIX MONTHS BEFORE MY SON lay in critical condition in a hospital in Tucson, we had celebrated his first birthday. As we waited for word from the doctors, I remembered Aaron, sitting in his high chair, petite, blond and wearing a pointy birthday hat, looking like me when I was a year old. He was completely immersed in cake and ice cream, smeared like a mask across his face. The high chair and the surrounding floor were a mess. He was all smiles and laughter.

Aaron stayed in the Tucson hospital for ten days. For the first three or four days, it was touch-and-go. But on the fifth day, he started to come around. He became more active to the point he was uncomfortable with all the wires attached to him. One afternoon he started to yank them off. We had to be vigilant to make sure they stayed on.

During those touch-and-go days, when Aaron's condition was critical, neither Donna nor I dwelled on the concern about the future or the possible outcomes of the illness. All we wanted was to have Aaron well and to come home.

Donna and I called our families to let them know how Aaron was progressing. I did not talk with my parents during this time. It was not until we saw my parents later in the year that we discussed Aaron being in the hospital. By this time, all was in the past. My parents had seemed apathetic about Aaron's health. At one point I joked with my parents, signing, *At least if he had become deaf I could sign to him and he would have grandparents to communicate with him.* We all smiled.

SETTLING IN TO TUCSON, Donna and I found a small two-bedroom house on Fifth Street across from Roschruge Elementary School and down the block from Tucson High School. While we were at work—Donna working as an administrative assistant in student housing at the University of Arizona, me at ASDB—Aaron was cared for by our neighbors, the Hochules, who had a daughter Aaron's age. After a year, we found a large, single mobile home on nearly two acres in Marana, Arizona, about a half-hour southwest of Tucson. I loved the rural environment. Our neighbors were at least a tenth of a mile off in any direction.

Once we settled into our new home, we had to find a school for Aaron. Desert Winds Elementary was about two miles from our house and provided a half-day kindergarten program. We had to decide between the morning and afternoon session, and chose the mornings because Aaron took a long nap in the afternoons. Once he was finished with his morning classes, he spent afternoons in an after-school program. It seemed I was settling into a life as a counselor, as a husband, and a father.

IN LATE SPRING, before school closed for the summer, I attended an American Deafness and Rehabilitation Association (ADARA) conference. ADARA is an organization for professionals who work with deaf people, providing various services such as, but not limited to, vocational rehabilitation, counseling, and job development. While there, I met Raye through professional circles. She, too, was from Tucson and was attending the University of Arizona's Rehabilitation Counselor for the Deaf program. We hit it off like we were meant to be.

When I returned to Tucson, I spent as much time with her as I could during the evenings, weekends, and vacations. We both had a common love for working with deaf people. She was a fluent signer. She knew I was married. Unlike the aromatherapy I tried in Bisbee, Raye seemed to fill a void. I cannot say I was especially proud that I was flirting, and Raye knew I felt conflicted. Although we were not sexually involved, I think we both suspected that it was only a matter of time. Our nonsexual relationship lasted two months. We both agreed that our current arrangement was not in either of our best interests.

Donna knew about Raye. To her, I minimized the relationship, insisting Raye was solely a friend and nothing else. Donna wasn't stupid, of course, but I didn't care what she thought.

When I said goodbye to Raye I was beset with loneliness. I felt even emptier than I had before. I found myself on edge much of the time. I noticed it over the next year, when Aaron was two, and I was focused on graduate studies and work. I was angry and lacked patience. I was never particularly physical with Aaron, but on occasion I would spank him. Most of the time, I just screamed.

One morning Aaron was not following the morning routine to ready himself for school.

"We're going to be late!" I screamed. "Hurry!"

Aaron ran through the house, oblivious to my directions. I grabbed him by the arms and shook him. "Get ready!"

This was uncharacteristic of me. He was startled and cried, quickly shaping up his act. As we drove toward town, I became overwhelmed with emotion. I pulled the car over and started to weep. I got out of the car to be alone. After a few minutes, when I had gathered myself, I climbed back in. Naturally curious, Aaron asked what was wrong. I told Aaron I was sorry for grabbing him and yelling at him. I'd chosen the wrong disciplinary method.

In an effort to shame me for my behavior, my father often yelled at me when I was a child and several times did grab me to put over his knee and spank me with a belt. Looking back, I might venture to say I was attention-deficit hyperactive or, perhaps, even a bit oppositional defiant. I would take things that didn't belong to me, disregard and disobey instructions, and fight with my younger sisters. I had a short attention span and was always running around with extra energy. I had difficulty concentrating in class, which resulted in my teachers frequently threatening to send me to the principal's office. I'd deliberately provoke my father by taking the candy bar he was planning to eat that night as a snack while watching television. It was not that I schemed to take his candy bar. I just did it without thinking.

As I self-diagnose, I can see that I exhibited many of the behaviors I see in kids I have counseled in school and in private practice. I explain to teachers and parents the need for students and children to focus on positive ways to manage their difficulties. That axiom is what I have lived and practiced for myself. I began to thrive in life when I was able to direct my energies in positive ways as an adult.

For the next couple of years, though, Aaron had to endure either my absence or my irritability. I was neither a good father nor spouse. I did love Aaron, but I was wrapped up in my own sickness of not addressing my issues of a failing marriage and the guilt of not being a good father. Aaron did not know what to expect from me from day to day. One day I'd be positive and loving, and the next I'd explode in anger. I was repeating my own father's erratic behavior, which I did not like, nor did I like myself. I sought out a therapist to address my behaviors and to work on my failing marriage. I hoped to resolve the issues that were threatening my marriage and attempt to reconcile with Donna. It was not only the arguing and bickering or the self-medicating or ignoring what Donna had to say; it was that over a long period of time I simply fell out of love.

In January 1987, I declared to myself, "I need off this emotional roller coaster." I could not keep Aaron and his mother on the edge any longer. I decided to find an apartment in town and file for divorce. Donna and I agreed that Aaron would live with each of us two weeks out of the month. Instead of making Aaron, who was six at the time, house-hop between the two of us, we kept the home in the country. Donna and I kept secondary living quarters for ourselves, but when it was our turn to watch him, we individually moved to the country home. We were trying to ensure some sort of stability for him. This also allowed Aaron to attend the neighborhood school without having to commute.

Aaron and I loved to hang out. We'd eat, watch movies, do homework, and read books. He was bursting with energy; often, I found him easier to handle if we were outdoors. Sometimes he'd get so wound up he'd drive me crazy. I'd grow irritated and impatient. And although I was never physical with him, with the exception of a rare spank, I was a terrific screamer. I'd learned from the best, my father.

AARON CAUGHT SIGHT of a fish.

"Keep the line in the water," I whispered. "Let the fish come to Aaron, not Aaron to the fish."

Aaron and I were fishing on a small creek in the Bighorn Mountains in Wyoming. The semester had ended for the summer, so I had taken time away from a tumultuous and draining academic year to take Aaron, my grandmother Richards, and her sister, my great aunt Inez, on a two-week road trip to Lovell, Wyoming, to visit my grandmother's cousin, Harold DeSpain.

During our stay, Harold led us on a daylong drive into the Big Horn Mountains, northeast of Lovell. We had geared up and taken the hour-long drive into the forest, all the while with Aaron jumping up and down in the back seat in excitement. The drive took us through canyons and up into the forests above the valley floor. At one point, Harold eagerly told us to look out the window on the driver's side. At first we could not see what he was looking at, but soon we saw a herd of wild horses running along the canyon just above the river that snaked through it.

Once we arrived at the small creek, Aaron spilled out of the car. "I want to catch some fish!" Harold was amused, watching my son's first fishing expedition.

"Here," I said to my son, "this is how you bait the hook." Aaron was so hyper, I was afraid he would hook himself. "Be calm," I said. "Here's how you use the rod."

Aaron laid his line in the water. We'd been through this several times. Each time he caught sight of a fish, he'd pull out his line and put it in again over the fish.

"Be patient," I reminded him.

He finally caught his first fish. He jogged over to show the fish to Harold, who congratulated him with a big, warm smile. That day, Aaron caught several more fish and was thoroughly proud of himself despite our having to throw them back because they were too small. It was the thrill of catching them that counted for Aaron.

IT DIDN'T TAKE LONG FOR MY SOCIAL LIFE to make a comeback after Donna and I separated. On March 20, 1987, a Coda friend of mine, Ed Gervasoni, who also worked in the vocational department at ASDB, had arranged one of his often-held parties. He usually invited about thirty people and the evening was filled with singing, drinking, dancing, and frolicking. One night, although I knew everyone going, I did not know whether I was up for it. Besides, I had to be in Phoenix the following morning. By the end of the workday, Ed had worn me down: I would go.

I was driving a multicolored 1963 VW bug that was so decrepit you could see the pavement through the floorboards. It was quite like a Fred Flintstone car; it would not have surprised me if one day I had had to use my own feet for momentum. I decided to stop at a liquor store to pick up a six-pack of Corona as my contribution to the party.

When I arrived, the party was in full swing. Music blared, couples danced. People had clustered together in small groups already deep in conversation. The apartment was small with two bedrooms and a bathroom off to the side of the living room and a kitchen in the back. I made myself comfortable, placed my beer in the fridge, and mingled. Ed threw his arms around me and hauled me over to formally introduce me to his roommate, Jennifer. She was a petite woman, about five feet two inches, and had lovely brown shoulder-length hair. She was very attractive. I had already met her at ASDB, where she taught in the elementary school and at various parent-teacher meetings, but this was our first social interaction.

To say the least, we hit it off. We talked about books we had enjoyed reading, gossiped about staff at school, and delved into spirituality. We discussed *Out on a Limb* by Shirley MacLaine. We stayed with each other the entire evening, dancing, drinking, and joking. We found ourselves alone in one of the rooms and sank into an intense dialogue. I was riveted by her intelligence and wit. I could not remember when I'd last had such a good time.

Because of my prior commitment to be in Phoenix the next morning, I had to leave. I promised Jennifer I'd call her. The following Monday I caught a glimpse of Jennifer entering a classroom and followed her. As I reached out to touch her arm, she shrank away. I was perplexed. It seemed she felt I'd blown her off when I didn't make good on my promise to call her. *Whoa,* I thought, *I just met this woman and already I'm in trouble!* Did I need to reconsider my attraction? I was too intrigued to step away. Luckily, I persuaded her to give me another chance, and we spent more time together. Soon we were dating steadily.

During our April break from ASDB, Jennifer and I made reservations to spend a few nights at Mormon Lake Lodge, a half-hour drive southeast of Flagstaff. We rented a one-bedroom cabin and disappeared. The days were warm and the evenings a bit chilly, in the thirties. One night as we lay spread out on a thick cushion of blankets, hypnotized by the flames of a fire in a pot-bellied stove, I blurted out, "I love you." I felt a flash of heat in me as I said the words.

Jennifer sat quietly for a moment, then smiled and hugged me. Later she would tell me that she, too, loved me, but that evening she had felt too insecure to share her feelings. She was treading carefully into the relationship, afraid of getting hurt. Jennifer and I now have this running joke that I loved her first.

AARON, NOW SEVEN, WAS A NERDY KID with a squeaky, high-pitched voice. His hair was short and blond and he was on the skinny side. He wore oversized glasses attached to a thick string to keep them from getting lost. Aaron did not lack in the ears department, and the glasses accentuated them. He was a highly personable character. He lived with Jennifer and me every other month, though he attended the elementary school near Donna in northwest Tucson.

Jennifer and I hit a few bumps in the road as we ventured into our life together. The first had to do with our ideas on how to raise kids. We'd grown up in completely different home environments. My parents had always been fairly permissive and discipline was lax or, at least, inconsistent. Also, Mom and Dad were never available; we simply didn't have a relationship, and they didn't participate in my life. Jennifer had grown up in a good Catholic family of three girls who largely stayed out of trouble and parents who moved a lot for her father's job.

Another challenge we faced as a new couple involved Donna, who as Aaron's biological mother spurred us all to come to consensus as to what Jen's role would be in regard to Aaron. We decided that Jennifer would serve as a "helper." Our biggest problem was figuring out how to accept one another's philosophy of discipline. It was a struggle for us, and we were forced to seek out professional help. Jen was highly disciplined, and I was more permissive. In the end, we met in the middle. I found this to be extremely difficult because I had not had an appropriate role model for becoming a balanced father, one who was even-tempered. I was inconsistent—like my father. I was a screamer—like my father. When all else failed, I screamed.

These behaviors were not helpful and, more to the point, they were detrimental. I did not like myself very much when I screamed and knew I needed to seek help to cease these angry outbursts. With much work, and as the years passed, my outbursts dissipated. Now, endearingly, I am accused of the occasional rant or rave. However, I continue to be conscious of my anger and that awareness helps me to control any potential eruptions.

Aaron was a lot like me when I was young; he was very independent and did as he pleased. One afternoon Donna called me frantically with news that Aaron was lost. We found out later that he and his friend had decided to leave the school premises for a few hours. When they returned, they were oblivious to the commotion they had caused. I saw a terrific reminder of my own oblivious, wandering ways as a child. Hadn't I too, as a toddler, sent my mother into fits by falling asleep in a bathroom cupboard and wandering down the street to spend the afternoon at the local precinct?

When Aaron was about nine years old, we transferred him from the elementary school near his mother to Brichta Elementary School because it was a two-minute walk from our house. At first, the transition to a new home and school went well. However, as the school year progressed, the calls increased from the school, as did those from his after-school program supervisors.

"Aaron is having difficulty completing his work," his teacher said. "He isn't participating in class, and on two occasions, he has fled the classroom."

The story was the same in his after-school program. He was having angry outbursts, and had run away from the program on at least one occasion. It wasn't anything we hadn't already glimpsed. When we tried to help Aaron with his homework, he would not hear of it.

I remember when I was in fourth or fifth grade, I had needed help with my arithmetic. My parents had told me, "We cannot help you. We do not know how to do the work." I was furious. I wadded up my paper and threw it on the ground. I don't recall ever asking them again for help with schoolwork. It so happened that, at the time, my parents had taken in a deaf foster teenager, and I was feeling neglected. I'm fairly sure it was their displaced attention that I needed, not help with my homework.

Like me, Aaron would hurry through his work so that he could go out to play with his friends. He did not save his antics for when he stayed with Jen and me; he was perfectly good at driving his mother crazy as well. I chuckle now, but back then, I used to say, "Phew, I'm glad he's with his mother." Donna said the same thing after her month with him.

Once, during a parent-teacher conference at his school, his teacher suggested that Aaron might have attention deficit hyperactivity disorder (ADHD). We certainly didn't reject the idea—we had already considered it—and I wondered whether he had some neurological damage from the spinal meningitis. His mother and I took him to a psychiatrist, who confirmed Aaron had ADHD. The doctor prescribed a medication, a stimulant that might counter his hyperactivity. The medication seemed ineffective. After several drug trials, we decided to stop using it. After all, I'd been a live wire as a kid, and I'd turned out all right. Maybe he inherited ADHD from me; we'll never know.

AS A PARENT, I had the advantage of being a therapist, counselor, and educator. I have done group work and work with individuals with ADHD and attention deficit disorder. Many have difficulties with making responsible choices and decisions. Sometimes their choices are not in their best interests. As a therapist and a parent, I had to make tough choices regarding my son's decisions. I did not want to enable him, but on the other hand I did not want to just allow him to sink. I had to find the right balance, and it took trial and error to find the right outcome for me as well as him. Now that I am older, I have to think about what my son will do or be when I am not present in his life any longer. Many parents want to see their children successful and at peace when they leave this planet, and I am no different. I want to feel that peace. It is difficult being a parent at times, and I wish there were a blueprint on how to make everything smooth and fluid. Perhaps this is what I had in mind when I thought I did not want to be a parent. Yet I made the choice to be a parent and, with all the trimmings, came that responsibility.

14
Claiming a Legacy

My grandmother's birthplace had been in ruins for over a half a century, but she could still remember the area. Granite is a small town in Utah just outside Salt Lake City, and the place where Grandmother Richards, my mother's mother, was born in 1905. It sits at the foot of the Wasatch Mountains. Together with my grandmother, who now lived in Mesa, Arizona, I drove with seven-year-old Aaron and my grandmother's older sister Inez toward Wyoming. Our route took us north through Flagstaff and into Kanab, Utah, with vermilion cliffs beckoning in the distance. In Granite, we visited a small cemetery overgrown with weeds and strewn with litter to see the graves of some of my ancestors from three and four generations ago. My grandmother was eighty-two now, and I felt certain this would be her last trip to her hometown. This was the woman who had helped raise me, and I was curious about where her home was located and what school she attended. It was a bit of a quest for us. She could give approximate locations, but the topography had changed over the years; sometimes we weren't quite certain of where we should go. Still, I felt excited just being in a place that was part of my family history.

As we journeyed north through eastern Idaho and along the Snake River, we arrived at the west entrance of Yellowstone National Park. Immediately, I found the place familiar from so many trips to see my grandparents over the years. I remembered the black bears that once climbed trees alongside the road, the herds of elk and bison grazing, the moose, and the foxes jetting across the road. Now the place was crowded with heavy, slow-going traffic.

When we arrived at Yellowstone's Old Faithful geyser, my heart quickened. I knew that Jen had passed through earlier in that same summer, the summer of 1987. She had hidden a note for me along a trail, under a rock. She'd sent me directions and I followed them precisely. I located the trail, counted off paces, turned to the right, found two pine trees, and lifted the second boulder to their left. Beneath, I discovered a love note in Jen's handwriting with an invitation for a romantic date in San Francisco at the end of my trip.

One evening thereafter, Jennifer and I ventured out to Tequila Mockingbird for happy hour in the El Con Mall in Tucson. The place was already crowded, and we were lucky to find a small table. We made small talk and then not-so-small talk. "I love you, and I want to marry you," I said.

She went completely silent. The room seemed to fall away. I could no longer hear the bar's commotion, the clinking of glasses, the boisterous voices. I waited. After what seemed an eternity, Jen cautiously asked, "You want to marry me?"

I'd taken her by surprise. "Yes, I want to marry you, will you?"

Her smile was delicious. "Yes."

In October we moved into the Drachman House, a small two-bedroom territorial-style house built in the 1930s. Its worn wooden floors and fireplace conveyed a cozy warmth. We loved it—for the time being, because it was very small. Unfortunately, when we refused to sign a two-year lease, we had to give it up. We then moved into a lovely territorial-style home on Fourth Avenue just up the street. We enjoyed the fact that it was only a two-minute drive to work and that twice a year we were right in the middle of the Fourth Avenue Street Fair.

Wedding plans were in the works. We decided on June 2, 1988, and appropriated the summer for a honeymoon in Europe. I felt fortunate having found a woman I truly loved. I know this sounds a bit hokey especially since this was my third marriage. Although Jen and I had crossed paths at the school before meeting, I knew I had fallen in love with her at first sight.

Because I had been married before in both a traditional church ceremony and a casual home setting, Jen and I agreed to find an alternative option. We did not want anything fancy or elaborate, so we decided on a justice-of-the-peace wedding. Jen's sister, Mary Anne, came for the wedding. A handful of close friends attended our ceremony at City Hall.

Jennifer curled her hair and wore a denim skirt and purple blouse. I wore my black jeans with an orange-and-black striped shirt. Justice of the Peace James West officiated our wedding. The brief ceremony took place during our lunch break from school, and afterward we returned to work for the remainder of the day. We celebrated in the evening at the home of friends. I was thrilled to have my sisters Kathy and Christy attend. My parents were on their Mormon mission trip to England, so they didn't come. I am sure my sisters told our parents that I was going to get married . . . again. But at this point, it was a nonevent. I wrote a letter letting my parents know about our trip to Europe and the approximate date we would visit them in England.

If the wedding was quiet and small, the honeymoon was its opposite. Our plan was to fly into Madrid, travel through the Pyrenees and down to Granada, and then travel to France, take a boat to Ireland, and end up in England.

In Madrid, we toured many of the fifteenth- and sixteenth-century cathedrals and the Museo del Prado, then we traveled to Barcelona. We trekked to Andorra and stayed at a pension in the village of Puigcerdà, sampling paella at a café where fish was served, eyeballs and all. From Andorra, we took a bus up the snaking mountainous roads, something we had tried to avoid because of Jennifer's motion sickness, but now was the only way to get there. From there, right along the mountain range between France and Spain, we backpacked up the mountain on a three-day hike. The first night we slept halfway up the mountain in a meadow surrounded by trees. We could see the lights of Andorra. In the morning we broke camp and made our way to Prat Primer, our destination above the tree line. We stayed in a shepherd's one-room brick building that had two metal beds and a fireplace. The mountain peaks majestically rising in every direction were covered in a June snow. The view of the plunging valley was breathtaking. The following morning, before the sun peeked over the eastern mountains, we began to make our way down the pristine mountain. By nightfall we had made it back to Andorra. From there, we took the train down the coast of Spain through Barcelona, the orange groves and olive trees of Valencia, and into Granada.

Walking back from Alhambra, the ancient Moorish fortress and palace complex, we discovered a school for deaf students. Eagerly, we approached what appeared to be the main office but found the door locked. It was late in the day, so we decided to return the following morning. "Hola," we heard when we arrived the next morning, discovering the doors open.

We entered, and Jennifer did most of the speaking, because her Spanish was better than mine. "What is your method of communication?" she asked the hearing teachers.

They replied that they used the Ling method of speech development, an oral approach to teaching language. At this time in the United States, many schools and programs for deaf children used ASL or various manually coded sign systems like Signing Exact English, while others used the oral approach. The oral-manual debate has been going on for centuries despite the overwhelming use of ASL in the Deaf community. We had the opportunity to share with the two teachers that Jennifer was a teacher for deaf children in an elementary school and I was a counselor working with children and adolescents from elementary to middle school. We explained that in our school we used Total Communication as a way of instruction, communicating in all possible modalities: writing, speech, and/or signing. The school was technically closed for the summer, so no children were present. We wished our Spanish was more fluent, which quite possibly would have extended our meeting with the two teachers. Still, we were very excited to have time with our peers in another part of the world.

"Is the school government-funded?" I asked, thinking of ASDB. This particular school was a private school in which families were responsible for tuition and fees. The school was similar to ours, with classrooms and a cafeteria but unlike ASDB, it was not a boarding school. The deaf kids lived in the area and commuted to the school. Before long, our tour and time came to an end.

AFTER WE LEFT SPAIN, we traveled to Paris and saw the Louvre and the Eiffel Tower. Then we took a train to Le Havre to catch a boat to Ireland. We had been on our honeymoon for about five weeks, and there had been recent signs that Jennifer was not feeling well. The white-capped seas of the English Channel made for rough travel, and she had severe motion sickness. The passage had not been easy on me either. I had managed, as long as I sat perfectly still near a window. I counted myself lucky that I fared better than most of the passengers.

All had seemed well after we disembarked at Rosslare Harbor, on the southeastern tip of Ireland. A short woman with salt-and-pepper hair curled atop her head held up a sign advertising "Mrs. O'Leary's Bed and Breakfast." It really was Mrs. O'Leary. We hopped into Mrs. O'Leary's small station wagon and she drove us up into lush green hills dotted with black-and-white cows. A few days later, we ventured west to the Ring of Kerry and stayed in a bed and breakfast hosted by the Ryan family. We had planned to stay just a night or two, but Jennifer was still not well. The family took her to the doctor, and the extra days we spent there they were attentive to her. But our sightseeing was cut short.

In Cork, we rented bicycles and stumbled upon a sign: Wanted: Deaf Laborers. It was tacked up on a business storefront under renovation. We stopped to peer through the window and saw ladders and paint buckets. It was exciting to see someone seeking to hire deaf people.

Later that evening I attempted several times to contact the person listed on the storefront sign. Finally, on my last attempt, a man with a thick Irish accent answered the phone. Excitedly, I explained I was a counselor and worked with deaf children in Arizona, and that my wife and I were on our honeymoon. I told him that we saw the sign looking for deaf workers. The Irishman seemed more reserved than me. Perhaps it was a cultural thing? Or maybe he wondered who why this stranger was calling him? Nevertheless, we agreed to meet the following morning at a café.

Despite the morning's chill, Jennifer and I scampered off to meet the Irishman, whose name I learned was Tony. He was of medium height with a sturdy build and casual dress. When we approached his table, he rose to shake our hands. He had a slight smile on his face, but other than that, he was all business. We introduced ourselves. Tony was a local businessman who had joined with other businessmen to set up a nonprofit enterprise that would teach and train construction skills to deaf people. After a hands-on training, the graduates would, with the help of Tony and his associates, find employment.

Tony explained to us that in Ireland the government was responsible for running the programs for deaf children in schools but did not include vocational training; individual communities assumed the responsibility for training deaf people in vocations. I explained how this was the opposite in the United States. The federal government gave money to states and local communities to help support schools. Some private agencies also taught vocational skills to deaf people. We discussed the programs at Gallaudet University that he might be interested in contacting, and I gave him the names of some individuals at Gallaudet as well as people in other states he might contact. During our conversation, Tony was all business. I wondered if he had parents, a sibling, relative, or friend who was deaf, but I didn't get the chance to ask though our meeting lasted several hours.

I look back and hope the information I provided helped Tony and the business community in Cork.

OUR NEXT STOP AFTER IRELAND was London, and then Birmingham, England. I knew my parents were there, but I wasn't sure how to find them because we didn't have the exact address, just the street name.

So we knocked on doors up and down the street. At last, someone answered the door. A petite, elderly woman stood in the threshold as we introduced ourselves.

"Do you know Mel or Eileen Sorensen?" I said.

"Yes, follow me," she said, and walked us up the street to a small, brown two-story row house.

I pounded on the door. Growing up, my parents had doorbell lights that would come on when someone arrived. But this house did not. So I knew I needed to create a vibration that they could feel inside the house. I went up to the windows to look in. The pounding eventually worked.

When my mother came to the door, our guide said, "Your parents are very sweet people. I find them to be a joy."

I signed to my mother to tell her that her neighbor thought she was sweet. My mother smiled coyly, in that same familiar way I had known all of my life.

We spent the next four nights with my parents. Jennifer had visited my parents a couple times in Fullerton. She and my parents got along very well, I think, and unsurprisingly, they liked the fact that she could communicate with them easily. Jennifer seemed at ease when signing to them. Whenever we visited my sister Lori and her husband, John, in Fullerton, my parents would come over to Lori and John's house. Jennifer and my sister Debbie always made it a point to sit with my parents and sign to them so that they could understand and participate in what was going on. My sisters and I always started out signing when our parents were in the room, but sometimes we stopped and just talked. It was just the natural rhythm of our lives together. However, Jen and Debbie always continued signing their conversations on whatever topic they were talking about. Jennifer oftentimes told me how enjoyable it was talking/signing with my parents.

In England, my father was sixty-five and my mom fifty-seven. My mother had recently retired from Hughes Aircraft in Fullerton, while my father had been retired for quite some time. And they were on a

Mormon mission that was the culmination of my parents' dedication to the church.

By the time we met my parents in Birmingham, they had been on their mission for nearly a year. The days we spent in Birmingham were gray, and it rained much of the time. We spent a few days touring the countryside. My father drove as my mother navigated. Driving on the left side of the road took some getting used to, and I was grateful I wasn't driving. During our short visit, we toured many castles and manors.

Our ancestral families lived in several of these manors, my mother signed. She did not know quite the details, but she knew the names of the families. When she was not doing her work with the Mormon Church, she often went to the libraries to research genealogy.

I found much more information in England than I ever found in the United States, she added.

I would have loved to live in England, my father signed. *To stay here. But the cost of living is expensive,* he told us.

I could see my parents were very happy. It was nice to meet them on neutral territory. After four days we continued our journey, this time to Scotland.

AFTER BEING HOME IN ARIZONA ONLY THREE DAYS, Jennifer became ill with severe cramps. We hurried to urgent care, where we learned that she was miscarrying. She had been sick twice during our stay in Ireland and again in London, but unaware that she was pregnant, we had thought nothing of it. Now it all made sense. We were grieved by our loss but accepted that this was meant to be.

Before our marriage, Jennifer and I had discussed quite extensively the possibility of having a child. This might sound rather odd or cruel, but I told Jennifer that although I would not mind having another child, I could not give fifty-fifty. In other words, she was going to have to do most of the work. I was already a father, and at age thirty-nine, I felt somewhat weary about being a father again. Also, as a counselor at ASDB, I felt, in an odd way, that I was a father to many of my students. Because they lived a long way from home, they often didn't see their parents for five or six weeks at a time, and that often left me playing the role of a surrogate parent. My lack of enthusiasm in wanting another child was not meant, in any way, to be neglectful or malicious; it was just how I felt. Jen didn't seem to hold it against me. But she hadn't given up her desire to be a mother. She let me know she wanted a child, preferably a daughter.

15
A Place in the World

In the fall of 1988, Jennifer became pregnant again, and this time we were both excited. Jennifer's excitement was contagious, to say the least. I now knew how much this meant to her. In preparation for our baby's birth, we researched child-birthing methods and decided on the Bradley Method, which was all natural, with the husband (me!) as the coach. We started a six-week class during Jen's fourth month of pregnancy. I decided I would be the best coach and father ever! So much for my fifty-fifty speech.

The Bradley Method emphasized the father's participation in the pregnancy and birth and discouraged the use of painkillers. We went to classes that not only focused on the actual moments of labor, but also taught the necessity of a healthy diet and moderate exercise throughout the pregnancy. I was involved 100 percent during Jen's pregnancy. Jen followed through with the instructions regarding diet and exercise. I cannot remember hearing about what my father did during my mother's pregnancies, but it would seem, in the 1950s, that the father's role in regard to childbirth was limited, and fathers were most likely not even permitted in the delivery room. Also, my mother was probably given medication to relieve the pain of childbirth. We were certainly going to take on this project in a very modern way.

At about 11:30 on the night of July 5, Jen said, "I think my water broke."

Sure enough, there was the telltale puddle of water on the floor of our bedroom. "We must call the doctor," she said. "Let's get to the hospital."

"It's nothing," I said. "We should wait until morning." In our birthing class our instructor had told us that when the water breaks, it's not an emergency, but rather, a time to prepare. Well, Jen won that debate, and we called the doctor to make reservations at the University of Arizona Medical Center. We arrived at around two in the morning. After checking in, Jen and I were shown to our room. She got comfortable in her bed. I got the chair, where I proceeded to sleep fitfully for nearly four hours.

"I knew this was going to be a bad idea," I grumbled. "Nothing is going to happen other than I'm going to get a bad night's sleep." Jen awoke around 6 or 6:30 . . . I was (still) awake. She still was not in labor, so the nurse told her to take a walk to stimulate the onset of labor. This worked and she began to dilate at a normal rate. The last hour of labor, when Jen was in extreme pain, I'd have happily resigned as her coach. I was blamed for getting her pregnant, which, to be fair, I did. I was criticized and rebuked for things beyond my wildest dreams. I'd never heard such words come out of Jennifer's mouth. She was, however, superb to me once in the middle of the intense labor. When the nurses were chatting about having lunch, Jennifer piped up and said, "Yes! Get something for David to eat!" The entire room burst into laughter. I was accorded a lunch by my caring wife.

I could see my daughter crowning. With each push I felt a wave of excitement course through my body. Kyla Cole Sorensen was born eight hours after the onset of labor on July 6, 1989, on her exact due date. Only Jennifer could orchestrate the timetable of her own daughter's birth.

THE BIRTH OF KYLA only heightened Aaron's need for attention. Aaron was nine years old and no longer the only child; he now had to share attention. To make Aaron feel secure, Jennifer and I both tried to balance our time with him. We also encouraged his participation with the new baby. We taught him how to bottle feed Kyla, and let him push her stroller when we went on long walks. If Kyla received any gifts, we made sure to give one to Aaron as well. We were vigilant in making sure that Aaron felt included.

Donna, Jennifer, and I decided that Aaron should join a baseball team. We thought it would be good for him. He'd learn self-discipline as well as teamwork. Jennifer and I attended most of his practices and went to each of his games. I was stalwart in my support, telling myself that I wanted to be involved, that I was not handing him off to be babysat by a coach. Always, in the back of my mind, I told myself that I would not repeat my father's mistakes. After a month of baseball, Aaron's interest waned. We tried to force him—to bribe him, even—to finish. We ended up losing that battle.

Another time, Aaron wanted to take karate lessons. As parents, we hoped this might be the solution. We went to karate class for about a month before, once again, he lost interest. I was beginning to see that Aaron was all about instant gratification.

With Aaron's ADHD and attention-seeking behaviors, he was becoming more physical with Kyla. Once when Aaron was eleven years old and Kyla was two, we'd just arrived home from picking up a pizza. I gave the pie to Kyla to carry into the house, but Aaron wanted to do the honors. With a hard push, he jerked the pizza out of her hands, and Kyla fell to the ground crying. That was the last straw for us. The following week, Aaron's mother and I agreed that Aaron would move into her home and visit us only on the weekends.

This didn't quite solve the problem, because now he had only the weekends to get my attention. It seemed to me that he felt he needed to compete with his sister for our attention and had ramped up his competitiveness. I know Kyla was oblivious to all of Aaron's bullying and other attention-seeking behaviors, but the whole dynamic gave me pause. I was very cognizant of dispersing attention between the two kids—toddlers naturally need more attention.

I, too, sought out the attention of my parents when I was young, but I'm also sure that sibling rivalry I had with my sisters was fairly healthy. Despite our in-fighting, my parents knew they could trust me with tending to them if they went out for the evening. Although there were times when my young judgment may not have been the best—as in the infamous diaper-changing fiasco—I cannot recall a time when I was malicious toward them. Neglectful, yes, distracted, yes. But it was not mean-spirited.

Aaron simply did not like school. After Brichta Elementary School, he attended Prince Middle School. Aaron's attendance at Prince was good; school seemed to be working for him. There were no significant behavioral problems. He had satisfactory grades. He even tried his hand at cross-country track, but, in true Aaron fashion, that lasted all of two weeks.

The academic part of school was difficult. By high school, it was a constant struggle for him. At one point, Aaron was tested and placed in the gifted program. Donna and I thought that there might be a chance for him to succeed in the gifted program, which was not as traditional as the other classes. We did everything in our power to keep him in school, and I never missed a meeting about him. At one point, I even accompanied him to his first-period class, German. I knew that it was only a last-ditch effort to keep him attending class, and sure enough, when I stopped going, so did he. He did not make it through his freshman year, and, at the age of fourteen, he left school altogether.

Aaron preferred to skip school, hang out with his friends, and run away from home. Each time his mother and I attempted to bring him back into the fold, he would take off for days and weeks at a time. However, most of the time we knew where he was living: with a female friend and her mother. All we wanted was to have him safe and with a roof over his head. Donna and I decided to give part of my child support payment to the family he was living with. There was no way he was going to come live with either of us. Besides, by now, Donna and I knew he was not going to finish high school.

It was not lost on me that I had been the same age when I moved into my grandmother's home in Joseph City. We were both at the age when we wanted our independence. However, Aaron followed a different path than I did. He ran away numerous times, while I did not. He moved in with another family, and I moved in with my grandmother. He blew off school, whereas I attended. Granted, the world was different in the 1960s than in the mid-1990s. I moved to a rural area, while Aaron lived in a larger city. I have always thought of myself as more street-wise and Aaron more naive.

A breakthrough of sorts presented itself when at age seventeen one of Aaron's minor scrapes with the law landed him in a detention facility. While in detention, he received his GED. It turned out that his class at the high school received diplomas only days after he received his GED. Aaron always had to do it the hard way, just like his old man. We both "made it," albeit the outcomes were different. I have always contended that if Aaron had remained home with Jennifer and me, the outcomes would have been entirely different.

Aaron was a gifted electrician, and work opportunities led him to live with my sister Lori and my brother-in-law John in California when Aaron was in his early twenties. The connection to his grandparents was tenuous at best, much like my own relationship with my deaf parents as an adult. Aaron had limited contact with my parents because he felt awkward about communicating with them. As Aaron was growing up, he had learned some sign language, but mostly the alphabet. He was not exposed to many deaf people. Although I would sign with him, it was infrequent. I neither encouraged Aaron to learn sign language, nor discouraged him. Part of the reason for this was that Aaron did not have as many opportunities for exposure to ASL. Aaron did not have the role modeling as Kyla did growing up with both of her parents fluent in ASL. While in California, Aaron had some contact with my mother, although their communication was restricted. His relationship with his grandparents came down to cordial visits where they would smile at each other a lot and fingerspell some words.

It was different for Kyla. Throughout her young life, she was exposed to deaf people. When she was in elementary school in Tucson, she had deaf babysitters. Often, when Jen and I entertained, there were many deaf individuals in our home. Jennifer and I always signed to her. While in high school, after we moved to New Mexico, Kyla took two continuing education courses in ASL at the University of New Mexico. Kyla's receptive and expressive signing skills are impressive.

JENNIFER AND I ENCOURAGED KYLA TO READ. We bought her books and read to her, but the reading habit didn't kick in until high school. Aaron had always been the opposite, reading voraciously from an early age. Kyla definitely took after me in the reading department. My father only read the newspaper, and I did not find out that my mother was a reader until I was in high school. The good educational head start that Jennifer and I gave her set her up well, but there would be some bumps in the road.

The year we moved to Albuquerque, Kyla went to two different schools for third grade. One day, she came home and announced to Jennifer that she had been put in counseling. We couldn't understand why we hadn't been informed. Upon questioning the school administration, we learned that Kyla was in counseling because of her behavior. Somehow by being extremely quiet, she had triggered a red flag. The school suspected that there were issues regarding "divorced parents." Jennifer and I looked at each other in bewilderment and shook our heads. Because Jennifer and I have different last names, the school had assumed that she had divorced parents. We pulled Kyla out of that school after six weeks.

Jennifer had taken a job at Zia Elementary School teaching blind students. She asked the administration if Kyla could enroll, to which they agreed. Kyla attended Zia for the remainder of the year. Unfortunately, despite the change in schools, Kyla was continuing to fall further and further behind. Although she was never in any trouble, we knew that she was too quiet, and nobody was noticing that she wasn't keeping up.

For fourth grade, Jennifer started looking for a private school for Kyla and stumbled across information about a Montessori school. Because the classes were small, teachers could give more attention to Kyla. We decided to give it a try, and much to our delight, it was perfect for her. The Montessori of the Rio Grande was hands-on and deliberately organized in their methodology. The environment encouraged Kyla to do her best. Parents were welcomed into the school and encouraged to participate in the many family-oriented activities throughout the school year.

Despite Kyla's lack of interest in books until high school, she was and is a visual learner; yet when it came to auditory learning, we noticed issues. When she was five, she started piano lessons and learned to read music in the traditional way. In her fifth year of piano

From left, me, Jennifer, Aaron, and Kyla in front of my home in New Mexico on Christmas Eve.

study, while living in Albuquerque, we heard of the Suzuki method in which a student learns an instrument by listening to music rather than reading it. Kyla was extremely frustrated with this method of practice. It dawned on Jennifer and me that she might have some auditory processing issues then. When we looked back at her academic history, we had been worried about these signs and shared our suspicions with her teachers, and they were helpful enough to modify her work. Over the years, Kyla had become highly resourceful in receiving and retaining information in school. On her own, she had developed a system of taking highly detailed notes. Kyla was organized and private, always knowing when her mother or I had looked in her backpack or folders. But then when Kyla was thirteen, we had her tested, and it was confirmed that she did have auditory processing issues. By then she was in the Montessori school, which further helped her develop the skills she already had cultivated.

At the Montessori school, Kyla experienced a period of stability, having the same teacher for three years before graduating and moving on to a charter middle school, Twenty-First Century, which also had small class sizes and which allowed Kyla to develop a true connection with her teachers. She blossomed, playing on the school basketball team and continuing to play community soccer. After middle school, she transitioned easily into Amy Biehl High School, another small charter school. Jennifer and I had hoped Amy Biehl would be the catalyst for Kyla to stretch herself in high school and push her limits. Kyla did just that, push and stretch.

Amy Biehl High School's philosophy is service learning. The school encourages its students to become involved and help out in their community. The teachers came to know Kyla very well, and she knew them quite well. Though Kyla was reserved, when she spoke out she made a difference. She had annual projects for which she had to make public presentations. During her senior year she served an internship at the Roadrunner Food Bank where she had to do a public presentation summarizing her experiences. It was awesome to see her growth during her four years at Amy Biehl.

By the time she graduated in 2007, Kyla had taken twelve college credits at the University of New Mexico, and she graduated in the top 10 percent of her class. Kyla emerged as a beautiful red and lightly scented carnation, ready to succeed in the world. She is now is an accountant at the University of New Mexico. She is married, and I am a grandpa.

I know that most of Kyla's success has been due to her mother's love of education and deep belief that children must be taught to become productive citizens. I believe Kyla to be truly insightful in her ability to recognize these qualities in her mother. Jennifer and I remained integral in her education, and Jennifer involved herself by sitting on the school board and participating in the parent organization.

Kyla also understands her father and his impatience with any kind of teaching. Luckily, I wasn't often called to assist her in her studies. In informal situations, we could spend hours discussing music, politics, education, and relationships. For years we had father-daughter

Top row, from left: My sister Lori, my daughter Kyla, my sisters Kathy and Christy. Bottom row, from left: My sister Debbie, my wife Jennifer, my niece Jessica, and my grandson Cooper.

days. Each Saturday we had lunch and took in a movie, just the two of us. Kyla and I are alike in terms of our habit to "cut to the chase and give me the information."

AS MY CHILDREN WERE STRUGGLING to find their place in the world, I was starting to find minc. In Nevada, I had had to work under the radar on Deaf advocacy issues, with much success consulting with legislators in establishing a charter school for deaf students in Las Vegas, even without my boss' support. Now I was the program director at Desert Hills for the NMHID in Albuquerque, New Mexico, where I was to develop a residential treatment program for deaf adolescents. I had to hire, provide training for, and supervise the staff, as well as provide therapy to the deaf students admitted into the program. Furthermore, I was in charge of marketing, as there was an expectation to not only sustain the program but also expand it.

The NMHID ran into financial difficulties about a year and a half after I was hired. My paychecks became sporadic. Jennifer started looking for part-time work. We struggled to make ends meet and found ourselves resorting to using credit cards to help with expenses. Eventually the NMHID filed for bankruptcy. Because they owed me several thousand dollars, I decided to file suit. I hired a fantastic gravelly voiced attorney named Wes, who was tall and thin and chain-smoked. While the lawsuit proceeded, Desert Hills began to financially back the program. They hired me to pick up where I had left off. When I won the suit, the NMHID was ordered to cover all my back pay and expenses I had incurred through the court proceedings. That award was enough to pull us completely out of debt.

I had always hoped that one day I would work for myself. I knew I had found my niche when I discovered how lacking New Mexico is in providing mental health services to deaf people. There are more than 5,000 licensed independent social workers, psychologists, and clinical counselors to serve a population of almost two million hearing individuals. That breaks down to one therapist for every 300 or 400 in need of mental health services. However, there are only two mental health therapists for several thousand deaf people living in New Mexico.

For seventeen years, I was the only fluent signer licensed to provide counseling to deaf people in New Mexico. On top of that, I was the only outside consultant who provided mental health consultation for the deaf to the Albuquerque Public Schools district. The New Mexico Division of Vocational Rehabilitation cannot refer outside agencies to deaf clients. Developmentally disabled deaf adults are a unique population in which significant behavioral issues arise due to communication barriers with hearing people. There is a severe lack of behavioral therapists who can work with this group of individuals. Those who have either private insurance or are on Medicaid have difficulty locating appropriate mental health services. My general experience with various mental health issues is extensive; however, my expertise is limited to several areas, of which I am ethically bound to inform my clients. I joke to my colleagues that I am a Jack of many trades and a master of few.

In 2000, I started a private practice, Southwest Services for the Deaf, which provided mental health therapy to deaf individuals and consultative services to private and governmental agencies. Southwest Services for the Deaf did not fill a gap, but rather a void. I obtained my city business license, tax identification code, and other necessary registrations. At the same time, I applied for my Medicaid number so that I could provide behavioral consultation to developmentally disabled deaf individuals on Supplemental Security Income or participants in long-term services, which equipped me to work with populations without a consultant or provider for services for deaf people. I became a vendor for the Division of Vocational Rehabilitation to assist their deaf clients in job-related services. I submitted a proposal to provide consulting services for Albuquerque Public Schools' Deaf and Hard of Hearing Program. I also applied to various insurance panels in order to work with private clients and submit third-party billing. I knew mental health services were limited in all these areas, and I was enthusiastic to take on the challenge.

When I had all my ducks in a row, I met with the CEO at Desert Hills to explain what I was doing: resigning my position to focus on my new business. I proposed that I work as an independent contractor to continue to provide mental health services for deaf people who were in the Desert Hills program and to continue helping with their marketing. There was initially some resistance, but eventually the CEO agreed to the contract. At this point I was doing everything from hiring to firing, training, supervising, marketing, and providing therapy to the students and families at Desert Hills. The expectations and responsibilities were overwhelming. I would still provide individual and family therapy as required, but my role of "doing everything" would be pared down to only consultation—and this "everything" allowed me to expand Southwest Services for the Deaf's role in the community and state.

BY THE SPRING OF 2002, I incorporated Southwest Services for the Deaf, and my goals came to fruition. I was now the consultant for the school district and had expanded my work with various state agencies and organizations. I obtained all my licenses to provide services to Medicaid clients as well as work those who are developmentally disabled. I was on my way. I expanded mental health therapy to many deaf people in New Mexico who otherwise received services through an interpreter. Having a third party interpret for the therapist is awkward, cumbersome, and much of the time, causes information to get lost. On top of that, many interpreters are not adequately trained in the mental health field. Also, when a third party is involved, confidentiality can become an issue. I do not mean to say there are no qualified mental health interpreters; there are, but they are few and far between.

I felt there was a need to expand treatment for deaf adolescents in the community. I wanted the treatment to be more community-based, replicating a homelike atmosphere. I envisioned the home to be fully accessible in every way possible. I felt it was essential that the home be managed and operated by an all-deaf staff receiving a living wage. I investigated nonprofit agencies who would invest time, energy, and financial resources. In the fall of 2003 I made contact with Ken Kinney, the development coordinator at La Familia Inc., a nonprofit that had begun by providing adoption services in the mid-1980s. The agency later expanded to provide not only adoption services, but also treatment, foster care, and other valuable services for youths and families.

I worked with Ken, who, in turn, worked with his board to get the approval to set up the group home. Despite the fact that La Familia is a small local agency with a small budget, it took the risk and rose to the occasion to help establish the first group home of its kind for deaf people. The doors opened within a year and a half to a select group of boys and girls ages fifteen to twenty. The Deaf Group Home serves as a step-down program for students who have gone through residential treatment in hospitals, offering them a less-restrictive environment to reintegrate into the community. While continuing the task of exploring and learning to manage their mental health issues, they acquire independent-living skills.

The older students attend one of three schools or participate in a transition program from school to work. They learn how to navigate the community by using local transit, become familiar with local resources that help them become successful in the community, such as the Division of Vocational Rehabilitation and the Community Outreach Program for the Deaf. Furthermore, they gain the confidence to access community college services, compete in competitive employment in Albuquerque, and transition to their own apartments.

Some of the students remain in Albuquerque after graduating from the Deaf Group Home, while others return to their home communities, which can be problematic due to a lack of services. Regardless of support, the transition process is slow. By applying what they have learned in the Deaf Group Home, they can begin to navigate their home communities. The program has worked with students from all over the United States, and Southwest Services for the Deaf contracts with La Familia to provide home therapy, interpreting, marketing, and clinical supervision.

My small, unique company has its fingers in many pies. We have consulted with various public agencies and organizations in New

Mexico, Arizona, California, Oregon, Iowa, Hawaii, and other states, and have provided education and training to professionals in the field of mental health.

Being a Coda definitely had its advantages during my career. My parents were well-known in the Deaf community and had many connections that were helpful in my work. My work at Desert Hills from 1997 to the present allowed me to meet other individuals throughout the nation at workshops and conferences. Through the years, Southwest Services for the Deaf has been recognized in the community. Whenever an agency in New Mexico or a parent from out of state needs advice on how to work with their deaf child or adolescent or where to seek resources within their state, it is not unusual that we get a phone call or an email.

One day, a family in Iowa called me about their thirteen-year-old adopted son who was deaf and had experienced shaken baby syndrome that left him blind and with significant brain damage. This is just one example of the many families needing resources who have sought me out through the years. As I often do, I asked the parents how they had come by my number. "We looked on your website and talked with other deaf professionals in the area," they said. "They recommended you by name." I told them more about what I did. They told me they could send all the paperwork, and they added they were ready to pull up stakes to move to Albuquerque so they could be close to their son while he worked with me.

"Can you help us?" they asked.

"Absolutely," I replied.

Epilogue

As a lifelong advocate for deaf people, one part of the job is to repeat myself early and often, educating and reeducating those who enter into a career involving deaf people. I find many entering into the field come off as hardcore zealots who believe they will be the voice for the Deaf community, as though deaf people could not speak or act on their own behalf. This thought in itself is oppressive.

My father was a leader in the Deaf community, just not in the same way I am. My advocacy for deaf people is through my work. His was to be a role model and to educate nondeaf people in the way he lived, through his church activities, and through athletics.

I see myself as standing in a lineage, privileged to have been born to deaf parents and to be there to bear witness to what has been accomplished for deaf people in this country. I don't want to lose sight of those victories. Since the beginning of time, the stronger people—whether in population or in muscle—have played the dominant role in shaping culture and determining the economics of who gets served and the politics of who has rights. Deaf people, like past immigrants to the United States, have been subjected to this paradigm: Chinese and Irish immigrants were forced to build the nation's railroads; Africans were stolen from lands afar to serve as slaves on plantations; Native Americans found their lands dispersed among the white population and were killed in large numbers. Deaf people, too, have been put into subordinate positions for thousands of years. During the time of the Greek and Roman empires, deaf people were not allowed to own property, go to school, or marry. Being deaf meant you were less than human, incapable of learning. Not until the eighteenth century did deaf people in Spain, France, and England find schooling opportunities and gain civil rights.

The nineteenth century ushered in formal education for deaf children. Two men in particular brought education to deaf children in America, Thomas Hopkins Gallaudet and Mason Cogswell. Cogswell had a deaf daughter named Alice and was concerned about how he was going to educate her. Gallaudet investigated the educational practices in France. On his visit there he learned a great deal about the education of deaf students and French Sign Language. He met a deaf man by the name of Laurent Clerc who also happened to be a teacher for deaf people. He then persuaded the man to move to America. They established the first permanent deaf school in 1817, the American School for the Deaf in Hartford, Connecticut. During the remainder of the ninteenth century a proliferation of deaf schools sprung up throughout the United States.

During the Lincoln administration in the 1860s, a new college opened, dedicated to the educational advancement of deaf students, and appropriately named after Thomas Gallaudet. By the early twentieth century, almost every state in America had a school for the deaf. Also, it became legal for deaf people to marry and hold property.

My purpose in writing this book is to lend my voice to the advocacy of improving the lives of deaf people and their families. I hope that in sharing the story about the changes during my lifetime, I have contributed to keeping the needs of deaf people paramount. I know that much has been accomplished because many people have advocated for better services. When I was a child in the 1950s, the only services provided to my parents came from my sisters and me. This was common for many deaf families with hearing children back then. My sister Debbie and I played the roles of interpreters, receptionists, and secretaries for our parents. As we did not own a phone until the 1960s, we relied on our next-door neighbors for use of a phone and for taking messages in case of emergencies. I was ten before I even owned a radio, and I played it so much that I broke the tuner. Of course, deaf people had no use for radios and often did not consider buying one for their hearing children.

My parents were like many other adults in the Deaf community in that they faced many obstacles to communication and relied on their hearing sons and daughters to mediate conversations with the hearing world. When they had news to share, they sometimes went overboard. I remember when my father bought his new 1963 blue Chevy station wagon, he was pumped and bursting with pride. Because Dad couldn't just get on the phone and brag to his friends, he decided he'd have to just show it off. One Saturday morning he piled the family into the station wagon and we drove to one of his friend's homes in the Los Angeles area to show him the new car. To everyone's chagrin he was not home, so off we drove to another friend's home. My father was bound and determined to show someone his new vehicle. Finally, we found someone home. Satisfied, Dad drove us home. Many times, for my parents, this was the only way to communicate.

"YOU ARE HEARING. What gives you the right to talk about Deaf culture?"

This question came from the back row of Deaf History 101, which I was teaching at Western Nevada Community College in Carson City, Nevada, in 1996. I was walking my class through the distinctions that define Deaf culture, especially their use of and pride in ASL.

That day in class I had described "Deaf Standard Time," the particular brand of those of us who are deaf and those of us who are part of Deaf culture when we run late. In the norms of Deaf culture, we have extended goodbyes, stay later, and arrive earlier. When the deaf find a deaf conversation partner, they are reluctant to walk way. It's not uncommon for me to find myself ridiculously delayed, for example, when trying to leave the office. First, Mary Anne needs to talk, then Bobby from across the hall, and invariably, Nancy, my deaf colleague, will send a shout down the hall, "David!" just as I'm about to escape into the parking lot. Of course, by the time I make it to the car, another teacher wants to confer about a mutual student, and before I know it, I'm an hour late. I often try to explain this to Jennifer, who is usually the one left waiting for me, but I don't think she finds it very endearing that I can't keep time, regardless of how I might explain that it is part of Deaf culture.

That student's question from the back of the room always burns me. My standard answer is, "I *am* Deaf culture, raised and given the cultural tools by my parents." To this man, on this day, I told my story this way. "True culture is handed down from generation to generation, but Deaf culture always has an element of acculturation," I said. "Deaf culture continually integrates aspects of other cultures to create its own."

The 1990s cemented the recognition of Deaf culture, in which the language, arts, expression, and customs flourished. The class wanted to engage with the question of whether Deaf culture would one day cease to exist. Possibly, but I doubt it. Although many cultures around the world become extinct, I'm fairly certain this will not occur for Deaf culture. The culture of deaf people is alive and well, constantly adapting. Like language, culture is fluid: it adapts, it morphs. Changes are positive. Without change, we stagnate and fail to grow.

A FEW YEARS AGO I gave a half-day seminar at Mental Health Services for the Deaf in Missouri on deaf issues and funding for mental health services for deaf people. Late in the afternoon session, a young woman asked about the lack of services and continued oppression of deaf people. The question was more of a statement begging to be answered. She was young, so I figured she must be new to the field and really had not understood the strides deaf people have made in recent years, so I answered, "No, deaf people have made significant progress over the past thirty years."

Briefly, I outlined what I had observed during my lifetime. We have technologies, programs for deaf people, ASL is a recognized language, along with culture, Gallaudet University saw its first deaf president, there are more charter schools at which parents have more options, and interpreter training programs to name a few changes. Is the playing field leveled? No, it still has bumps and dips that need to be graded. The woman at the seminar asked a valid question we should keep asking. But I have also been witness to the transition.

I SEE MYSELF AS A MEMBER of the Deaf culture/Coda transition generation. Recently I was talking about this with my friend, Tupper Dunbar, who is a Coda, too, and works as an interpreter.

"What do you mean, transition generation?" he said.

"I see that we are the link," I said, "between our fathers' generation of traditional deaf folks and the new generation of deaf students."

Tupper's experience as a Coda is somewhat different from mine. He and his family are Native American. They've lived much of their time in rural areas. As for me, my experience emanated from urban California. Put simply, I was the city mouse and Tupper the country mouse. Nevertheless, the two of us have unmistakably shared numerous experiences, which in the end all add up to traversing a similar culture: attending Deaf clubs and churches, participating in deaf sports, learning ASL as a first language, interpreting for our parents, and understanding the stereotypes surrounding Deaf culture.

"Our generation of Codas holds the key to the past traditions of Deaf culture," I said. "We are the last of the storytellers; we are the transmission generation. The current generation of deaf people have not heard firsthand what it meant to be deaf in the time of my parents. Yet, today's deaf citizens have reaped the benefits of what my folks and many deaf leaders have worked long and hard for."

Back then, the residential school was at the center of Deaf culture. Even on vacation, it was not unusual for deaf people to visit the state school for the deaf in a state as they were passing through because they wanted to connect with each other. Deaf schools were the centerpiece of social life, where young deaf students could get together and mingle. Sporting events brought deaf people in from all over the community. Weekly clubs for the deaf, another integral part of the culture, were attended by deaf adults and families.

When I cast my gaze on this culture, I want to keep it alive. So many younger deaf people already have schools, agencies, and training at their service, but what they don't know and what I want them to understand is where their culture finds a place in the world. Their culture is flourishing in different ways now. Yet culture always expands. Even the language itself changes.

The road to civil rights for deaf people has been a long and winding road. That is the prehistory of Deaf culture, and it's important to understand it, because culture is fluid. We must understand the past to see the future.

Up until the mid- to late-twentieth century, deaf people could not use a telephone, and all television and movies were "silent" for them, unless they went to the Deaf club to watch a captioned film. In the early 1960s, my father put in a lighting system throughout our house. Different lights flashed for different situations: if someone rang the doorbell, if the phone rang for the TTY, if one of the babies was crying, if noise was coming from the crib.

Today, deaf people enjoy all sorts of telecommunication technology: captioning for television and films; video relay services for home and office as well mobile video relay so that deaf people can communicate with hearing people; videophones, FaceTime, Skype, and other programs for face-to-face communication; sophisticated computer hardware and software; internet services and social media such as YouTube, Facebook, vlogs and blogs, Twitter, as well as email, text, and instant messaging, all of which can be accessed via smartphones on the go. With the use of these technologies, communication barriers for deaf people have mostly fallen away.

Another distinction between my parents' generation and today's lies in the role they played in their schools. Many early deaf leaders in the Deaf community were raised in residential schools. Deaf students gained experience in leadership roles as student body presidents or secretaries and team captains for the basketball and baseball teams. Today, many deaf students who are mainstreamed miss out on these opportunities because they are outnumbered by hearing peers at public schools.

Residential schools for deaf people still exist in most states; however, many have closed due to financial problems caused by the enactment of laws that require children to be educated in the least restrictive environment and by changing values. Most deaf children are now mainstreamed into public schools; only a small number still attend residential schools. In recent years, due to new charter school legislation, charter schools for the deaf have been established. These charter schools allow students to live at home and still have the benefit of learning in a deaf environment. The schools place a lot of emphasis on new assessment tools and stronger parent/sibling involvement. Typically these schools are for elementary and middle school students, with much smaller class sizes.

In the early 1990s while I was working at ASDB, Arizona enacted new charter school legislation. I jumped at the opportunity to establish a charter school for deaf kids from kindergarten to third grade. Emily, the mother of a deaf ASDB student, offered to help me. After presenting the idea to an organization of hearing parents of deaf children, I was met with a seventy to thirty vote for support—not bad, considering the novelty. Emily and I proceeded to obtain an application and other materials needed to develop a proposal for the State Board of Charter Schools. We understood that the charter school was an opportunity to implement creative academic models that would encourage academic achievement; parental involvement in their child's education; engagement with siblings; development of new assessment tools; programmatic enhancements, including ASL classes at school and at home, as well as learning to use the community as a classroom. I sat down with the principal of ASDB to have a heart-to-heart. I told her it might seem like this was a competing program, but the way I see it was offering more choices. The agreement I asked her to make with me was that I would never promote the charter school to ASDB families. My way of looking at it proved to be true, because the additional services helped many students and families, without hurting the existing program.

I did the bulk of the writing and used Emily as a sounding board, editor, and cowriter. We also recruited another deaf individual from the University of Arizona to work with us. It took a year and a half from the time we submitted our proposal to open the doors of

Laurent Clerc Elementary School in Tucson. No operation is without its glitches. ASDB staff was mixed in their response to the concept and development of Laurent Clerc. Some were unhappy that the new charter school was not buying into the old philosophy, which supported only residential schools. Others held the misconception that the new school would become an ASDB competitor. Luckily, enough people thought the idea of a charter school was wonderful to keep us encouraged.

Unfortunately, a conflict arose between the individual from the university and me. He wanted the full glory of saying the school was "his idea." Because I was the initiator of the project, I have to admit my ego was bruised and my feelings were hurt by this man's selfishness; the only reward I wanted was to see these deaf students succeed. However, the conflict raged, and knowing, ultimately, that I would not be around to see the doors open, I politely resigned from any involvement with Laurent Clerc. When I moved out of state, friends kept me informed of the school's progress, and I was disappointed (but not surprised) to learn that within a few years Laurent Clerc closed its doors due to poor management and in-fighting among staff.

In addition to the charter schools, deaf people now benefit from more community programs that provide interpreter referral services, job development and occupational-readiness services, and community awareness classes. Most states have commissions or boards that advocate for deaf people, along with nonprofit agencies dedicated to the Deaf community. The mental health field has expanded in many areas with treatment centers, group homes, and outpatient services. Although deaf people are still underserved in many capacities, fifteen years ago there were no residential treatment centers or group homes for deaf people and few outpatient services. Today, community colleges and four-year universities throughout the United States provide interpreting services for deaf students, and there are more than 125 interpreter training and deaf studies programs.

Yet I cannot overemphasize how abysmal mental health services in the United States are for deaf individuals. There are only a handful of private practitioners, hospitals, and group homes for adolescents.

Most kids receiving mental health services are in schools for the deaf where they are qualified only to provide education, not mental health care. Independent-living programs for deaf people are scarce. Often when deaf people seek out these services, they are denied because agencies do not want to pay the expense of interpreters. When agencies do accept deaf clients, the costs for interpreters are exorbitant, not to mention that the interpreters are not always qualified. Although many agencies say they have signing staff, all too often the signers know only a few signs.

Having outlined the many differences between past and current generations, it is even more apparent that Codas like Tupper and I and deaf people have the valuable responsibility of keeping alive the traditions of the past in the world of the present. Although technology has made things easier, it is healthy for deaf people to interact and excel within their own communities, to continue to develop Deaf culture, never disregarding where we have come from and how we got here. It is also critical that deaf people continue to make strides in the hearing world, demanding that schools, clubs, and medical services are as accessible to them as to those who hear.

I am thankful to be in the transition generation. I was able to take all of my experiences and create Southwest Services for the Deaf. Because of my unique upbringing, I feel that I truly understand the exceptionality of deaf individuals and how imperative it is that they have access to outstanding supplementary services from the community, whether they live independently or in group homes. I believe if it's out there, it can be found. And if it's not, it can be founded. I will always seek out the next agency, state or local, profit or nonprofit, that can offer the best to this extraordinary community. I will always be on a quest to expand services for deaf people, so long as I live.

Acknowledgments

I WANT TO thank the many people for their help, encouragement and writing support. Thanks to Deirdre Mullervy, Katie Lee, and Ivey Wallace for their work at Gallaudet University Press.

I want to thank Barbara Pritt for her stern assistance in seeing what I did not, when I needed to find my path back home and my path forward.

I want to thank my son, Aaron, and my daughter, Kyla, for being so much a part of my writings; my parents, Melwin and Eileen, who provided many lifelong experiences; my sisters, Debbie, Kathy, Christy, and Lori, for their perspectives.

Thanks to Carolyn Flynn, my Albuquerque editor. Without her encouragement, this book would not have been possible.

I especially want to thank my very significant other, Jennifer Cole. Without your support, numerous readings of my manuscript, and hours spent editing (and re-editing) all of this would not be possible, love.